AMERICAN HISTORY STORIES

VOLUME IV

AMERICAN HISTORY STORIES

VOLUME IV

BY

MARA L. PRATT

YESTERDAY'S CLASSICS

CHAPEL HILL, NORTH CAROLINA

This edition, first published in 2007 by Yesterday's Classics, is an unabridged republication of the work originally published by Educational Publishing Company in 1891. For the complete listing of the books that are published by Yesterday's Classics, please visit www.yesterdaysclassics.com. Yesterday's Classics is the publishing arm of the Baldwin Project which presents the complete text of hundreds of classic books for children at www.mainlesson.com under the editorship of Lisa M. Ripperton and T. A. Roth.

ISBN-10: 1-59915-205-3
ISBN-13: 978-1-59915-205-9

Yesterday's Classics
PO Box 3418
Chapel Hill, NC 27515

CONTENTS

ABRAHAM LINCOLN

ABRAHAM LINCOLN

Abraham Lincoln was the President during this dark time in our nation's history,—the Civil War.

He was not a handsome man, not an educated man, not a society-mannered man; but a more honest, more loyal-hearted, more grand-souled man than Abraham Lincoln, never stood at the head of our government. He was as honest as George Washington, as sturdy as Andrew Jackson, as brave as the bravest General, and, in the end, as noble as the noblest martyr.

He had had a hard life as a boy. He had been brought up on a Kentucky farm, where he had learned to hoe and to plant, to drive oxen, to build log-houses, to split rails, to fell trees;—everything that a farmer boy away out in a new country would have to do, this boy had done. Indeed, when he was named for President by the Republican party, the opposing parties sneered at him, calling him a "vulgar rail-splitter," "an ignorant boor, unfit for the society of gentlemen."

But for all his hoeing and his rail-splitting, for all his poverty and his hard labor, for all his rough home and his common companions, Abraham Lincoln soon proved that he had a something in his head and in his heart that any gentleman might well have been proud to own—a something that a world of fine houses and fine clothes could not buy— something which, by and by, prompted him to set all the poor black men and women free.

LINCOLN'S FIRST HOUSE IN ILLINOIS

Although Abraham Lincoln did live in the backwoods, and did not go to school, nevertheless, he was all this time in the best of society. Fortunately for him, his mother was a real lady in heart, and tried always to keep her boy from growing up a coarse, ignorant "rail-splitter," as his party opponents called him. She taught him always to keep his eyes open, and his thoughts awake to the beauties about him in nature. She taught him that it was a noble heart that could see God in the beautiful flowers, in the birds, in the fields, in the forests, and in the waters; that it was the artist's soul that loved to watch the beautiful sunset lights and the deepening shadows; she taught him to read the few books that she owned, and helped him to earn a few more; she encouraged his love for reading, and was careful that his reading was always of the best kind.

The result was, that when Abraham Lincoln came to be President, and had to write letters and make speeches, he always had the very best style of English at his command. When he said a thing, it was so simply and so correctly said, that every one knew just what he meant. And behind his words, too, there was always his big, honest, truthful heart. Is it any wonder, then, when, by and by, this good man died—shot down by an enemy of our Union—that all the country mourned for him, and felt for a time as if no one could be found to fill this good, great man's place.

Here is what a good woman says of him: "When Abraham Lincoln wrote a thing, you read what he meant. The meaning was not covered up under a heap of useless words. One thing was apparent in him from boyhood. This was his straightforward truthfulness and sincerity of purpose. No political experience ever twisted him; he ended life as he began it, an honest, sincere, trustworthy man. One of the great outcries against him by his opponents after he was elected was, 'He is an uncouth, rough backwoodsman. He is *no gentleman.*' It is true that he was very uncouth in face and figure; never handsome to look at, although the soul of the man sometimes shone through the plain features in a way that transfigured them, and his deep gray eyes were full of a great sadness, that seemed almost to prophesy his tragic fate. He had not the manners of a court, but he did deeds from the promptings of a simple, manly heart that a king might have been proud to own, and if he was not a true gentleman, God does not make many now-a-days."

When the Republicans chose Abraham Lincoln, the South was furious—not because they had chosen Lincoln, because they had chosen any one at all. "If a Republican President is elected," said these Southern States, "we will go out of the Union."

Now, it is said that the Southerners really were in hopes that a Republican President would be elected, so that they might have an excuse for leaving the Union. "We will go off by ourselves," said one of the Southern leaders, "and build up a government of our own; and we will have slavery for its very corner stone." They were very angry, these Southern slave-holders; for one reason, because they were now made by the United States Government to pay such high prices for slaves. One slave-dealer said, he wasn't going to pay a thousand dollars for a slave in Virginia, when he could go to Africa and buy better ones for fifty dollars a head! What do you think of a business that employed agents to catch colored men and women as you would catch animals, bring them into market, and sell them at a price, according to their size, or weight, or age, or strength for work!

We ought all to be glad that the United States Government at last came to its senses, and made all the States give up this wicked traffic.

Lincoln was in due time elected President, and the Southern States, as they had threatened, declared themselves no longer members of the Union. They made for themselves a new government, put Jefferson Davis at its head as President, and called themselves "The Confederate States of America."

JEFFERSON DAVIS

These Southerners believed that, although the States had all at one time banded together under one government, still each State had a right to step out and set up a government of its own if it chose. This is what John C. Calhoun said in his speeches before Congress, and without doubt he believed what he said was true. This was the same old question of "State rights" of which you heard away back as far as when Washington was President. Don't you remember how jealous of each other the political parties were even in those early times? How afraid one party was that too much power would be given to the central government, that is, to the President and Congress? And how equally afraid the other party was that the power would be too much scattered around among the different States? And do you remember in Jackson's administration, that some of these same Southern States declared the central government "null and void," and said they had a right to leave the Union if they wanted to? They even went so far as to form a league, and would really have made trouble enough had not Jackson rushed down upon them before they had time to do any mischief.

Here was this same old question up again, in a new dress to be sure, but it was the same old question.

The Northern people had no idea how much this matter meant to the Southern people. Even when South Carolina really "seceded" from the Union— even then the Northerners thought it was only a threat.

But lest we should be too severe in our judgment on these Southerners, let us stop and see why it was they cared so little about that "Union," which, to a Northerner, is so dear. This is the reason: the Southerner had been brought up from his babyhood to love his *State*, his *State flag*, his *State Government*. To him, his *State* was everything. He had been brought up to say, "I am a Virginian!" or "I am a South Carolinian!" It was his *State* flag that he had seen raised on festal days; it was the *State* flag that waved over the public buildings, and over their forts. Everything to him was State! State! State! He loved his State, he was proud of her, and he was ready to die for her.

Now let us see how the Northerner had been brought up. He, I am inclined to think, hardly knew what his State flag was—he never heard anything about it, never saw it. It was always the "Stars and Stripes" that floated before him in these Northern States. "The Star Spangled Banner," "My Country, 'tis of Thee," "God Bless Our Union," were the songs he had always sung. He never said, "I am a New Yorker!" or "I am a Rhode Islander!" but always, *"I am an American!"* Everything to him was Union! Union! Union! He loved the Union, he was proud of her, he was ready to die for her. So you see, these two parties could not understand each other. The Northerner could not believe that the Southerner would do such an *awful* thing as to break up the sacred Union, and the Southerner, on the other side, could not see that there was anything awful at all in breaking up the Union, which to him was not sacred at all.

LINCOLN IS MADE PRESIDENT

While this quarrel was boiling and bubbling, the day was drawing near when Lincoln was to take his place at the head of the nation.

He started from his simple home full of hope for his country, even in so threatening a time as this; full of honest intention to serve her faithfully, and with no wish to wage war upon any State or States. Innocent in his own heart, free from all malice, he could not believe it when he was told that a plot had been laid to murder him as he passed through the city of Baltimore. It was too true, however; and the friends of the new President found it necessary to have him pass through this city at night, under the cover of darkness.

On reaching the capital, he made his inaugural address, as all the Presidents have done since the time when Washington made his from the balcony to the people on the green below.

This address was honest and manly, as everything that Lincoln said was sure to be. He told the South that he had no wish to make any trouble for those States, no wish to interfere with their rights; he only desired that they should abide by the laws of the country. He said, however, that they had no right to withdraw from the Union, no right to take into their own hands the forts or any other property belonging to the Union; if they did these things, it was his duty, as the chief officer of the Government, to demand that they return to the Union, and give up any property they had taken.

Now, as both these things had already been done in the South, that party at once said, "Lincoln has no right to say we *shall* stay in the Union; we will *not* give up the forts that are on our own coasts; we will fight for them; we will not be ruled by any Union Government." And now the war was close at hand.

"FORT SUMTER"

MAJOR ANDERSON

During the last months of Buchanan's administration, Major Robert Anderson, who held command over the forts in Charleston harbor, had asked over and over again for men and provisions for these forts. He had shown the President plainly that he could not much longer hold them against the "seceding" States, unless help were given; but still no help had come. When Lincoln became President, Anderson asked again. Lincoln replied that help should at once be sent. The leaders of the "Confederates" or "Seceders"—you must remember both these names, for they both mean the Southern people—the leaders of these Southerners, hearing of this, went to Major Anderson and ordered him to surrender the fort to them it once.

Anderson, of course, refused. He knew only too well that he had no men, guns or powder with which to hold the fort, if the Confederates saw fit to fire upon it; still, loyal Unionist that he was, he determined to hold out to the very last. "It shall not be said that the Stars and Stripes are hauled down without a struggle," said he.

FORT SUMTER

He had only eighty men, but he thought he could hold out as long as the provisions lasted, and so this little band prepared for action.

There were three more forts in the harbor, all in Confederate hands, and beside this, they had built two great rafts upon which they had fixed cannons. These they floated round in front of the fort, and on *Friday, April 12, 1861,* the Confederates opened fire from these five points, all upon the one little fort with its eighty men. The "Civil War" had begun.

Down came the rain of shot and shell, around the fort, across the fort, into the fort. The wooden barracks inside took fire again and again; and on the second day, they were burned to the ground. It was a hot time for the brave little garrison. The air was so hot, and the smoke was so choking and so blinding, that they could work only with their faces covered with wet cloths. Every hour the fort grew to look more and more like a great ruin.

FORT SUMTER AFTER THE FIRING

It was plain enough that Major Anderson must surrender. All this time, however, the Stars and Stripes had been kept flying from above the fort. Even when they had been torn down by the flying balls from the enemy, some man had always been ready to nail them up again. But now the white flag of surrender had to be shown. The firing ceased, and the Confederates came over to the fort in boats to make terms with Major Anderson. It was agreed, after long discussion, that Anderson and his men should be allowed to march out with flying colors, should be allowed to salute the dear old flag with fifty guns, and then should march away in peace.

This was done; and as soon as they had gone, General Beauregard, the Confederate leader, marched into the ruined fort, tore down the "Stars and Stripes," and ran up the South Carolina State flag in its place.

This is a brief story of the bombarding of "Fort Sumter." Not a single life was lost on either side; but if millions upon millions of lives had been lost, there could not have been greater excitement throughout the country. Ask your fathers and your mothers, or your

THE SOUTH
CAROLINA FLAG

grandfathers and your grandmothers, to tell you about it. It was less than thirty years ago, and anywhere you can find men and women who remember those early times of the Civil War.

They were exciting days indeed! The different political parties of the North, forgetting all differences, all ill feelings, all quarrels, now joined hands and hearts in this terrible time. There was but one cry in the hearts of all—"Save the Union! Save the Union!" Nothing more was to be heard about Democrats or Republicans, tariff or no tariff,—Unionists or Confederates were the words now on every lip. No longer was it Republicans against Democrats, but the North against the South, the South against the North.

And now, President Lincoln sent forth a call for help—for men to go against the South. Seventy-five thousand men, he asked for, to help him "to preserve the Union." From every city, and town, and village, answers came. It seemed as if every man in the country was ready. Rich men and poor men marched away together side by side; willing to bear all the hardships of the soldiers' lot.

The women, too, were as alive as the men. It seemed as if the Revolutionary spirit had revived again in them. No woman was too rich or too poor, too high or too low, too strong or too weak, not to do something for the Union soldier. Little children, too, caught the spirit of the times. When they saw their fathers and their big brothers march away, their little hearts were full of tears, I fear, but they were all the readier to work for the soldiers because their own dear ones had gone away with them.

In the South the same feeling of loyalty to what they believed was right was shown among the men and women there. Remember they loved their States as truly as the Northerners loved the Union.

When the news that Fort Sumter had fallen into their hands was heard throughout the South, men and women were wild with joy. Songs were sung, verses were written, public meetings were held, and the South was boiling over with excitement.

Such was the excitement in the North and in the South after the taking of Fort Sumter by the Confederates. Let us see now what next was done.

THE FIRST
BLOODSHED

Do you remember what happened in the Revolution on one 19th of April?

And now we have another 19th of April to learn about—19th of April, 1861.

In answer to Lincoln's call for seventy-five thousand men, many a small company from the different States had been got together, and were training for service. One of these companies, the "Sixth Massachusetts Regiment," reached Baltimore, on its way to Washington, on this morning of the 19th of April, 1861. When the cars which brought them reached the city, it was met by a crowd of angry people armed with sticks, and clubs, and guns—a blacker, angrier mob was never seen.

These cars were drawn through the city from one depot to another, the soldiers inside. The mob followed, throwing stones and brick-bats into the windows from every side.

At last, unable to endure it any longer, the officer, ordered the soldiers to form into ranks, and march in a solid column to the depot.

PASSING THROUGH BALTIMORE

On they marched, the brick-bats and balls whizzing about their ears. Just as they reached the depot, the command was given, "Fire!"

Then the troops turned their guns into the crowd; and many a man fell before the fire of these soldiers whom they had attacked. For a moment there was a lull! The mob itself stood still before its awful work! But only for a moment; then with yells of rage and threats of revenge, they fell upon the troops, surrounded the cars, filling the air with howls and curses. Amid this terrible scene the cars rolled out of the depot. Three of the soldiers had been killed, and there were eighteen wounded.

FEDERAL HILL

During all this time the Confederates had been threatening to attack Washington, and tear down the Union flag from the Capitol. They had even said they would yet have their own flag waving over Faneuil Hall in Boston. Think of it, imagine anything but the "Stars and Stripes" waving over that old "Cradle of Liberty."

Even then the Northerners did not realize how full of hate the Southerners were. Washington was indeed poorly guarded, but the idea of attacking the Nation's Capitol! It didn't seem possible. But now there came a cry, "Washington is in danger! Help, help for Washington!" And help came. The Seventh Regiment of New York, a regiment of young men, kept up to this time only for parades, never expecting to be called into real war, came forward and *volunteered*, that is, offered to go to protect the capital.

How the people shrank from accepting this noble sacrifice! This pet regiment of the State! made up of the very "flower of volunteer troops," as it was said then, to go into battle to be shot down, very likely, like dogs! But they were ready; the country needed them, and so, one morning in April, this regiment marched down Broadway, the main street of New York city, to the cars that should carry them to Washington.

That was a great day in New York city! Crowds and crowds of men and women filled the squares and the sidewalks, and cheers upon cheers rent the air as these boys marched down the street. Theodore Winthrop, one of the young men in this noble regiment, in writing of this day, says:

"It was worth a life, that march. Only one who passed as we did through that tempest of cheers, two miles long, can know the terrible enthusiasm of the day. We knew now, if we had not known before, that our great city was with us as one man, united in the cause we were marching to sustain."

This regiment was joined by the Eighth Massachusetts Regiment, with General Benjamin F. Butler as one of its volunteer generals. It was supposed that General Butler had always had much sympathy with the South, and had been always in favor of allowing the South all the freedom to carry out their own ideas that could possibly be given them without real harm to the Government. But, when the South set out to break up the Union, no one rose quicker in its defence than did General Butler. When one of his Southern friends told him what the South was planning to do, Butler said:

"If you do that, I trust you are ready for war."

"Pooh! the North will not fight," said the Southerner.

"The North *will* fight," replied Butler. "You touch the Union flag and you'll find that the North will rise in a solid body against you; and if war *does* come, down will go your Confederacy, slavery and all."

But the South did not believe it, although they had good reason to know that General Butler had a "long head," as we often say when we mean that a person understands what he is talking about. Imagine their surprise then, when they found that even Butler himself was against them, when it came to be a real question with him whether to stand by the South, or to stand by the Union. Alas! it took the Southerners a long time to understand what the *Union* meant to a Northerner. And, alas, it took the Northerners a long time to understand what the *State* meant to the Southerner. It proved a bitter, bitter lesson to them both.

These regiments, the Seventh New York and the Eighth Massachusetts, arrived safely at Washington, and the capital was safe. But on account of the Secessionists in Baltimore, these troops had been obliged to get to Washington in a very roundabout way, to avoid being attacked as the Massachusetts Sixth had been.

"Now," said Butler, when he had fairly got his regiment in order after their march, "the city of Baltimore must be taken. The city is made up of Union men and women, but they are kept down by the few "Secessionists" there. That city must be freed. We can't bother to take our troops around through the woods and up the rivers every time we want to bring them to Washington, when there is a railroad straight through that city. No, Baltimore must be taken; and I will go and take it!"

Accordingly, he marched to Baltimore; and one night, when the sky was black and the rain was pouring, the wind howling, the lightning flashing and the thunder mumbling and rolling on every side, up he marched with his men and his cannon to the top of Federal Hill. There he was when the morning dawned, his flags flying, his guns ready, his great black cannons looking down upon the city as much as to say, "Make one move against the Union, lift one finger against our troops, and our black throats are ready to pour out fire and death upon you."

The Secessionists understood the language of the cannons, and from that time the Union soldiers marched in peace through the city of Baltimore.

THE CONFEDERATE STATES

The States that first withdrew from the Union were States farthest removed from the North. These States supposed that all the other slave States would at once join with them in their Confederacy. Those States which were farther

THE CONFEDERATE FLAG

north, nearer the Northern States, had more of the neighborly feeling than the first seceding States had ever dreamed of. In those States, Unionists and Confederates dwelt side by side, and in their legislatures, Unionists and Confederates voted side by side. So you see it was not so easy after all to pass "Secession" laws in these States.

Virginia was the first State to join the seven that had banded together to form their Confederacy. "Hurrah! hurrah!" cried the Confederates, "Virginia, Old Virginia, Virginia the mother of the Presidents, the home of George Washington, has joined us!"

But the Confederate joy was dampened a little when the western part of Virginia rose in rebellion, and said she would not belong to a secession State. This western Virginia held meetings, withdrew from the State, appealed to Congress, and, as a reward for her loyalty to the Union, was set off a State by herself, known ever after as "West Virginia."

Soon Arkansas joined the Confederacy; then followed North Carolina, then Tennessee. It is believed that Tennessee would not have seceded, had the Unionists not been threatened with "bullets and cold steel" if they dared say one word against the South, in the convention which was to be held in that State.

Kentucky and Missouri wished to have nothing to do with either side. They would stand by the Union, but they would not fight the South. Maryland, awed by the prompt action of Butler, was kept in the Union. Delaware, loyal little State that she was, and cautious too, preferred to stay where she was in comfort, rather than to join so uncertain a movement as this surely seemed to be.

The Confederacy then stood as follows:

These were the States that had left the Union and were ready to fight for their State rights, as they believed them to be. These were the States that had hauled down the "Stars and Stripes," and had hoisted in its place the Secession flag.

SEVEN ORIGINAL SECESSION STATES.

SOUTH CAROLINA.
ALABAMA.
GEORGIA.
MISSISSIPPI.
FLORIDA.
LOUISIANA.
TEXAS.

THE LATER STATES.

OLD VIRGINIA.
TENNESSEE.
NORTH CAROLINA.
ARKANSAS.

THE SOUTHERN CONFEDERACY.

SOUTH CAROLINA.
OLD VIRGINIA.
GEORGIA.
TENNESSEE.
ALABAMA.
ARKANSAS.
LOUISIANA.
FLORIDA.
NORTH CAROLINA.
MISSISSIPPI.
TEXAS

President of the Confederacy JEFFERSON DAVIS

YOUNG COLONEL ELLSWORTH

A ZOUAVE

There was a great deal of threatening all this time against the Union troops if they should *dare* set foot upon the "sacred soil of Old Virginia" as the Southerners called it. But for all that, the Government saw fit very early in 1861 to send troops into that very State.

The "New York Zouaves," led by Colonel Ellsworth, were the first to enter. The young colonel was handsome, and brave, and daring; and his troops, dressed in brilliant uniforms of red and yellow and blue, were the pride and delight of the army.

Ellsworth's troops entered the town of Alexandria, beyond the Potomac in Virginia, full of life and hope, and full of faith in their gay young colonel. On they marched, their colors flying, the drums beating, straight up to a hotel from whose top was seen a secession flag.

"Halt!" came the command as they reached the hotel entrance. Rushing into the building, up the staircase, he pulled down the secession flag, and marched with it down the stairs again. But at the foot of the stairway, stood the tavern-keeper, ready to resent this insult to his flag. Bang went his gun, and young Ellsworth fell dead. Bang! went another gun, and down by Ellsworth's side dropped the tavern-keeper, shot dead by one of Ellsworth's men.

I cannot tell you what excitement the death of this young colonel caused throughout the North. Every honor was paid him; every school-boy was told of the martyred Ellsworth; little babies were named for him; little boys were dressed in Zouave suits in imitation of him, and everywhere the name of Ellsworth was a household word

CONTRABANDS

There were many forts up and down the coast that had been taken by the Confederates; and there were others, still held by the United States Government, which the Confederates were equally anxious to get into their power.

To one of these, Fortress Monroe, Butler had been sent with troops. As soon as he had settled in his new quarters, Butler began to make short marches here and there about the country, that, by and by, when the people round about should rise against him, he might have some sort of an idea what kind of a place he was in,—where the roads were, where they led to, where the villages were, and how many people were in the villages.

Everywhere he went, he was met by negroes, who, when they saw his Union soldiers, would come up to them singing the funniest old songs, all about freedom, bondage, and the year of jubilee. Negroes, you know, are always a jolly class among themselves, always dancing, and singing their strange old tunes. These negroes, too, in spite of all their years of slavery, were still full of noise and music. Some of their songs are very funny, both in words and tune; others are so sad and weary; they speak to you of those dark, dark days when these poor men and women worked like cattle through the long hot days, were whipped and driven like cattle, and were bought and sold like cattle in the market place.

It began to be a serious question what to do with these negroes. The object of the war was not to free the slaves, but to preserve the Union. Many a soldier, many an officer in the Union ranks, believed yet in the right of the South to keep slaves if she wanted to. They were fighting only to save the Union. Others there were, who declared slavery a wicked sin; and these men claimed the right to save these slaves and free them.

But now the slaves themselves began to ask, "Are you coming to free us, or are you not?" And no one was quite ready to say.

The negroes supposed they were to be freed; and frequently slaves came into the Union camp, begging to be carried away somewhere, anywhere, only to be free. What to do with them was getting every day to be a puzzle.

Again General Butler came forward. "What shall we do with these negroes!" said he; "why, it's plain enough. The Southerners have always said these slaves are their property just as their horses and their cows, their tobacco and their cotton are their property. Very well! then we are to treat them just as we would treat the cows and the horses, the tobacco and the cotton—that is, we will take them for our own use.

That is the rule in war, that on entering an enemy's country, the army shall take everything it needs for its own use. Those things which the enemy takes are called "contraband goods." Therefore, since the negro is the property of the Confederate, we may take him just as we would take a Confederate Barrel of flour. He is, like the flour, contraband goods."

Nobody could find any fault with this, certainly. It was true enough. And after that the negro was called the "Contraband."

THE CONTRABAND OF PORT ROYAL

1. Oh, praise an' tanks! de Lord He come To set de peo-ple free; An' mas-sa tink it day of doom, An' we ob ju-bli-ee. De Lord dat heap de Red Sea waves, He jus' as 'trong as den; He

2. Ole mas-sa on he trab-bles gone, He leab de land be-hind: De Lord's breff blow him fur-der on, Like corn-shuck in de wind. We own de hoe, we own de plow, We own de hands dat hold; We

3. We pray de Lord: he gib us signs Dat some day we be free; De Norf-wind tell it to de pines, De wild-duck to de sea. We tink it when de church bell ring, We dream it in de dream; De

4. We know de prom-ise neb-ber fail, An' neb-ber lie de word. So like de 'pos-tles in de jail, We wait-ed for de Lord: 'An now he o-pen eb-ery door, An' trow a-way de key; He

say de word; we las' night slaves: To-day, de Lord's freemen.
sell de pig, we sell de cow, But neb-ber chile be sold.
rice bird mean it when he sing, De ea-gle when he scream.
tink we lub him so be-fore, We lub him bet-ter free.

CHORUS.

De yam will grow, de cot-ton blow, We'll

hab de rice an' corn: Oh, neb-ber you fear, if

neb-ber you hear De driv-er blow his horn.

SILVER BELL.

A NEGRO'S ANSWER

While the Union soldiers were in the slave States, the negroes, although most of them were at heart with the Union cause, had to be very careful what they said.

The answers, these negroes would make when asked which side they were on, were often very laughable. You see, there were so many spies around, that the poor negro never could be sure whether it was a Unionist or a Confederate that was talking with him. And he knew well enough that if he should make a mistake, and tell a Confederate he was a Unionist or if he should tell a Unionist he was a Confederate, he might be shot down.

One day, a gray-haired negro was seen perched on the top of a rail fence watching the soldiers with great interest. One soldier, thinking to have some fun, called out to him:

"Well, uncle, are you for the Confederates or the Yankees?"

A smile lit up his weather-beaten face, as he replied:

"Why, you see, massa, 'taint for an old nigger like me to know anything 'bout politics."

The soldier said rather sternly: "Well, sir, let me know which side you are on, any way."

The old man kept up his smile for a moment, and then putting on a grave look, which was quite laughable, answered:

"I'm on de Lord's side, massa, and he'll work out his salvation; bress de Lord."

"BIG BETHEL" AND "LITTLE BETHEL"

With Butler at Fortress Munroe, was young Theodore Winthrop, who, when his regiment was no longer needed at Washington, had offered to join Butler's regiment and go to Fortress Munroe.

From one of these Contrabands, Winthrop had learned that about two thousand Confederates had encamped at two churches called "Little Bethel" and "Big Bethel."

Butler and Winthrop at once began to plan an attack upon these Confederates. Their plan was this: the troops were to be divided into two bodies and fall upon the Rebels at Little Bethel, close around them, and prevent their getting to their companions at Big Bethel.

The two lines marched out quietly in the darkness, and came upon Little Bethel as they had planned. But here a terrible mistake took place. Just as these two lines met near the church they fired into each other's ranks, each thinking the other line the enemy. A scene of confusion followed and before orders could be given, the soldiers at Little Bethel had fled to those at Big Bethel, and together they were ready to rain down their hot fire upon the Union ranks. A quick hard fight, followed; and Winthrop himself, while mounted on a log to cheer his men, was shot dead.

Again there was mourning throughout the North that so promising a young officer should have fallen. The names of Ellsworth and Winthrop have always been held in respect; and for many a day were household words; until the time came when officers and men fell so thick and fast they could hardly be named or numbered, and their losses were known only in the hearts of their own friends, and in their own homes.

BETHEL

We mustered at midnight, in darkness we formed,
And the whisper went round of a fort to be stormed;
But no drum-beat had called us, no trumpet we heard,
And no voice of command but our colonel's low word,—
      "Column! Forward!"

And out, through the mist and the murk of the moon,
From the beaches of Hampton our barges were borne;
And we heard not a sound save a sweep of the oar,
Till the word of our colonel came up from the shore,—
      "Column! Forward!"

Through green-tasseled cornfields our columns were thrown,
And like corn by the red scythe of fire we were mown;
While the cannon's fierce ploughings new-furrowed the plain.
That our blood might be planted for Liberty's grain,—
      "Column! Forward!"

Oh! the fields of fair June have no lack of sweet flowers,
But their rarest and best breathe no fragrance like ours;
And the sunshine of June sprinkling gold on the corn,
Hath no harvest that ripeneth like Bethel's red morn,—
      "Column! Forward!"

When our heroes, like bridegrooms, with lips and with breath
Drank the first kiss of Danger, and clasped her in death;
And the heart of brave Winthrop* grew mute with his lyre,
When the plumes of his genius lay moulting in fire,—
      "Column! Forward!"

Where he fell shall be sunshine as bright as his flame,
And the grass where he slept shall be green as his fame;
For the gold of the Pen and the steel of the Sword
Write his deeds—in his blood—on the land he adored,—
      "Column! Forward!"

And the soul of our comrade shall sweeten the air,
And the flowers and the grass-blades his memory upbear;
While the breath of his genius, like music in leaves,
With the corn-tassels whisper, and sings in the sheaves,—
      "Column! Forward!"

                —A. J. H. Duganne.

---

* Major Theodore Winthrop fell while cheering on his men
and was left on the battle-field. Lieutenant Greble was also
killed in this battle.

DIXIE'S LAND AND JOHN BROWN'S BODY

In any war, each side has always some one piece of music which its armies delight to march by. An English Army, I presume, would march to "God Save the Queen;" a French army to the "Marseilles Hymn;" a German army to "The Watch on the Rhine."

And so in this war, each side had its own music. The Confederate army's especial favorite was "Dixie's Land;" while the Union soldiers delighted in "John Brown's Body lies a moulderin' in the Ground," or "Rally 'round the Flag, Boys."

I think you boys and girls ought to know these songs as well as to know the battles of the war; anything that helps to give us an idea of the thought of the people at a time, is a part of the history of that time. For this reason, I hope your teacher will find time to let you sing these songs now and then.

THE BATTLE CRY OF FREEDOM

1. Yes, we 'll ral- ly round the flag, boys, we 'll ral- ly once a - gain,
2. We are springing to the call of our brothers gone be - fore,

CHORUS.

Shouting the bat- tle cry of Free-dom, We will ral - ly from the
Shouting the bat- tle cry of Free-dom, And we 'll fill the va - cant

CHORUS.

hill-side, we'll gath-er from the plain Shouting the bat- tle cry of
ranks with a mil-lion freemen more Shouting the bat- tle cry of

Fortissimo.

Free-dom. The Un -ion for - ev - er, Hur-rah boys, hur-rah!

Down with the trait-or, Up with the star, While we ral -ly round the

flag, boys, ral - ly once again, Shouting the bat-tle cry of Freedom.

BATTLE OF BULL RUN

The Confederates had camped at a railroad junction in Virginia, where the railroads running west and those running south met. It was, as you see, important that such a place as that should be kept out of the hands of the Confederates, lest all means of railroad travel for the Unionists be cut off. The railroad leading direct to Richmond, the city which the Confederates had made the capital of their Confederacy, led from this junction. Because of this, the Confederates were carefully guarding this junction.

General Beauregard, the same Confederate who had ordered the attack upon Fort Sumter, was in command here. He was an odd looking little man, with snapping black eyes; and snow white hair. He hated "Yankees" as he hated rats; and used often to say, "We'll whip 'em, boys, if we have nothing but pitchforks to do it with."

The Confederate army was camped by the side of a stream called "Bull Run." With Beauregard was another general of whom you need to know, General Johnston.

General McDowell was coming with the Union army to meet this foe. At nine o'clock one Sunday morning, the armies met, and a terrible battle followed. The Confederates began breaking up and giving way. It seemed as if victory was to be on the Union side. But General Jackson turned the tide—Jackson, the cool-headed, iron-hearted, immovable Confederate General.

"Boys, there stands Jackson cool and firm as a stonewall!" said a soldier, as he saw him in the midst of this fearful slaughter, sitting as quietly upon his horse, giving his orders as coolly, as if he were in the quiet fields of his own plantation.

"STONEWALL" JACKSON

"Jackson like a stone-wall," flew along the lines, from mouth to mouth, and ever after this grim old general was called "Stonewall Jackson."

At noon time, fresh Confederate forces came up, and the already exhausted Unionists rallied to fight again. Back and forth the lines surged against each other. Guns were taken and retaken over and over. No one could tell which side was winning.

All this time, the Confederate leaders had been watching for new troops which were expected every hour from the Shenandoah valley.

The Shenandoah troops arrived! Woe, woe to the Union lines! the first knowledge they had of their new foe, was the yell that arose from every side, "The enemy are upon us! the enemy are upon us!"

Now followed a terrible fright. The Union soldiers, frightened and confused, dropped guns, knapsacks, everything and fled;—fled like wild animals with no reason and no order.

On, on they ran towards Washington, frightening the villagers as they passed along, calling to them to run for their lives from the foe behind. It was one of the most disgraceful flights ever known in history; and when it became really known what had been done, the North was indeed filled with shame and despair.

Here are two little stories connected with this battle of Bull Run, which although not what some people would call "real history," will help you to remember the battle.

Several dwelling-houses stood within the limits of the place where the fight was hottest, among them the house of Mrs. Judith Henry. Not suspecting that it was to be the scene of a battle, the family remained in the house until it was too late to escape. The noise of the battle came nearer and nearer, and soon cannon-shot began to plow up the ground around the house. Mrs. Henry, who was an invalid, was carried by her son and daughter to a gully, or kind of hollow washed out by running water, and there the three lay in safety until the army had passed by. Thinking themselves safe, the children bore their aged mother to the house again; but the Union troops were driven back, and the fight again raged so hotly around them that it was impossible to leave. The old lady lay there amid all the remaining terrors of the day; the house was riddled with balls, and when the tide of battle had rolled on, she was found so badly wounded that she died soon after.

EDDY, THE DRUMMER BOY

One of the saddest stories of the war is the story of Little Eddy, the Drummer Boy.

His father, a Union man of East Tennessee, had been killed, and his mother had gone to St. Louis with Eddy, then about twelve years old, in hope of finding a sister who lived there. Failing in this, and getting out of money, she applied to the captain of one of the companies in the Iowa First to get Eddy a position as drummer boy. The regiment had only six weeks longer to serve, and she hoped that during that time she might get work for herself and find her sister. The captain was about to say that he could not take so small a boy, when Eddy spoke out, "Don't be afraid, captain, I can drum."

Upon this, the captain replied, with a smile, "Well, well, sergeant, bring the drum, and order the fifer to come forward."

The fifer, a lank, round-shouldered fellow, more than six feet high, came forward, and bending down with his hands on his knees, asked, "My little man, can you drum?"

45

"Yes, sir," said Eddie, "I drummed for Captain Hill in Tennessee."

The fifer straightened himself up and played one of the most difficult tunes to follow with the drum; but Eddy kept pace with him through all the hardest parts and showed that he was a master of the drum.

"Madam, I will take your boy," said the captain. "What is his name?"

"Edward Lee," she replied, wiping a tear from her eye. "Oh! captain, if he is not killed, you will bring him back with you, won't you?"

"Yes, we'll be sure to bring him back. We shall be discharged in six weeks."

Eddy became a great favorite with the soldiers; and the tall, lank fifer used often to carry him "pick-a-back" over the hard roads and muddy places.

After the battle of Wilson's Creek, little Eddy could not be found. By and by the corporal, who had been searching for him, heard the sound of his drum not far away.

The company was to march away in a very few minutes, but not liking to leave the little fellow, the corporal went to find him.

He found him sitting up against a tree, looking deadly pale.

"O corporal, I am so glad you came! Do give me a drink of water! You don't think I'll die, do you?

That man lying there said the doctor would cure my feet."

Poor little Eddy! both feet had been shot off by a cannon ball. Looking around, the corporal found a Confederate soldier lying dead not far from Eddy. He, poor soldier, although he was himself dying, had crept up to Eddy and tried to bandage the little boy's feet.

While Eddy was telling the story, a Confederate officer came up and took the corporal and his little friend prisoners.

Very tenderly the officer lifted Eddy upon the horse before him, and started for the camp; but before they reached it, the little drummer boy was dead.

TENTING ON THE OLD CAMP GROUND

1.   We're tent-ing to-night on the old Camp ground, Give us a song to
2. We've been tenting to-night on the old Camp ground, Thinking of days gone
3.   We   are tired of war on the old Camp ground, Many are dead and
4. We've been fighting to-day on the old Camp ground, Many are ly-ing

cheer.   Our wea-ry hearts, a song of home, And
by,   Of the lov'd ones at home that gave us the hand, And the
gone,   Of the brave and true who've left their homes, Oth-
near;   Some are dead, and some are dy-ing, Ma-

CHORUS.

friends we love so dear.   Many are the hearts that are weary to-night,
tear that said "good-bye!"
ers been wounded long.
ny   are in tears.

Wishing for the war to cease, Many are the hearts, looking for the right, To

see   the dawn of peace. Tent-'ng to-night, tent-ing to-night,

last time pp.

Tent-ing on the old Camp ground, Dying on   the old Camp ground.

48

THE SEA-ISLAND COTTON PLANTATIONS

GEN. G. B. MCCLELLAN

After this defeat of the Union forces, the South was in high spirits. They thought the war was as good as ended in this one battle; but they did not know, as well as they did later, what the Northerners were made of, if they imagined one defeat would make them give up the "Union."

These soldiers, who had enlisted only for three months, were now, many of them going home; but other troops were pouring in from every town and village of the North. The North was indeed awake now. Now a great army was raised, and put under the charge of General McClellan, one of the finest military officers of the war. He very soon got his army into such fine order that they moved about as if they had been brought up, every one, from babyhood, in battle lines. This army was called the "Army of the Potomac." The only fault that was ever found with this army was that all this long fall and winter the army lay idle, except for two or three little battles of no great importance.

Every evening, as the Northerner sat down to read his evening paper, he read, "All quiet along the Potomac." This was well enough for a time; but as week after week passed, the North began to complain. Still, all remained "quiet along the Potomac"—until at last the very sound of the sentence came to excite indignation and anger among the waiting Northerners.

THE PICKET GUARD

"All quiet along the Potomac," they say,
    "Except now and then a stray picket
Is shot, as he walks on his beat to and fro,
    By a rifleman hid in the thicket.
'Tis nothing; a private or two now and then
    Will not count in the news of the battle;
Not an officer lost—only one of the men,
    Moaning; out all alone the death-rattle."

All quiet along the Potomac to-night,
    Where the soldiers lie peacefully dreaming;
Their tents in the rays of the clear autumn moon
    Or the light of the watch-fires are gleaming.
A tremulous sigh, as the gentle night-wind,
    Thro' the forest leaves softly is creeping;
While stars up above, with their glittering eyes,
    Keep guard—for the army is sleeping.

There's only the sound of the lone sentry's tread
    As he tramps from the rock to the fountain,
And he thinks of the two in the lone trundle bed,
    Far away in the cot in the mountain.
His musket falls slack; his face dark and grim,
    Grows gentle with memories tender,
As he mutters a prayer for the children asleep,
    For their mother—may heaven defend her!

He passes the fountain, the blasted pine-tree—
    The footstep is lagging and weary;
Yet onward he goes through the broad belt of light
    Toward the shades of the forest so dreary.
Hark! was it the night wind that rustled the leaves?
    Was it moonlight so wondrously flashing?
It looks like a rifle! "Ha, Mary, good-by!"
    And the life-blood is ebbing and plashing.

All quiet along the Potomac to-night—
    No sound save the rush of the river;
While soft falls the dew on the face of the dead,
    The picket's off duty forever.
                  —E. E. BEERS

"THE SEA ISLANDS"

But while this army is keeping so "quiet along the Potomac," let us take a run out into the ocean, and see what the United States Navy is doing all this time.

At the beginning of the war, the President had ordered that all Southern ports be blockaded. This was very necessary, in order to cut off trade between these ports and foreign countries. You can see how impossible it would be to starve out a prisoner if some one all the while were bringing supplies; so with the Southerners,—the quicker and more wholly they were cut off from all help, the quicker they must give way, and the sooner would the war end. Several vessels were sent to these different ports to blockade them; that is to keep any vessel from going in or coming out. One fleet was sent to the Sea islands, a group of islands south of South Carolina, that State which had begun the war against the Union. These islands produce the very finest cotton in the world. It is known in the cotton-markets all over the world as the "sea-island cotton." You can see now why it was important to get possession of these islands; at any rate, why it was important to shut them off from foreign trade.

The flag-ship in this fleet was called the "Wabash." Behind her were forty-eight gun-boats and steamers, and twenty-six sailing vessels. Quite a fleet, compared with that of 1812.

The commander formed his fleet into a big circle, and began to steam round and round between two important forts, all keeping up a steady fire as they passed round. Round and round they went, worrying the two forts on all sides, until they gave way—and the richest lands of the South were in the hands of Union vessels.

The owners took to flight, burning their stored cotton as they went, determined that not one shred of it should fall into Yankee hands.

The negro slaves did not flee. They came down to the water side as the vessels drew near,—some of them with the few little things they owned tied up in little bundles,—and begged to be taken away to the land of freedom.

In a few months, great changes were seen on these sea islands. The Yankees were busy learning to raise cotton, and everywhere were schools and teachers for these black people. Think of it! schools for the negroes! Why, the Southerners would as soon have thought of educating their cows as of educating their slaves.

SEIZURE OF MASON
AND SLIDELL

The president of the Confederacy, Jefferson Davis, was anxious to get letters to France and England, asking them for help. Of course, with the ports blockaded, it was almost impossible for any one to get away. But some way, two men, Mason and Slidell, did "run the blockade," went to Havana, and from there boarded an English vessel.

A Union sea-captain had heard of the departure of these two men, and, thinking they were up to mischief, watched them. When he found they had gone on board this English vessel, bound for England, he followed, came up with the English vessel, boarded her, and took Mason and Slidell prisoners as traitors to their country.

At first it seemed a very fortunate thing to have kept these two men from going to France and England with their letters asking for help; and the whole North was delighted. No one once thought that the English government had now a chance to say, "You have done to one of our vessels just what you waged war with us for doing in 1812. Have you forgotten that it was because of our taking men from your vessels that that war was brought about? Why can we not wage war upon you now for having done the same thing?"

No one thought of this; but England thought of it, and said it, too, very soon. She demanded, too, that the two men taken from her vessels be returned.

Some Northerners were at first inclined to stand by their deed; but there was an honest man at the head of the Government all this time, you know, and he said, "It does seem a pity to let these men go; but England is right, and it is our duty, not only to return the men, but to make an apology for taking them."

And when the people thought it over, they owned that England *was* right, and the two men were returned.

This was a good, honest, straightforward way to do, and I'm sure England and France both thought so, and respected the North for it. At any rate, the two men had no sort of success in either country, and the South was disappointed and disgusted with the whole affair.

THE MERRIMAC AND THE MONITOR

During the second year of the war, there appeared in the ocean not far from Fortress Monroe, a strange looking monster. Big, and black, and shining— what do you suppose it was?

It was an iron-clad war vessel which had once belonged to the United States Navy. The Confederates at the beginning of the war had sunk this vessel in the harbor; but afterwards some one had thought it would be a good idea to raise the hulk, and fit it up for a fighter.

They found, on raising this hulk, that it was firm and strong; so they had put a great iron roof over the deck, slanting it so that balls would glance off and so do no harm, had plated her sides all over with iron, and put on a great beak of iron and wood, making her indeed a most terrible looking enemy.

Down came this iron vessel straight upon the good old "Cumberland." Of course, no wooden vessel could stand an attack from this iron monster. For two hours these two vessels fought, although the Cumberland knew there was no hope. Bang went the cruel iron beak into the sides of the wooden Cumberland; and at last she sank, carrying with her her brave commander and his men, every one of whom fought to the last, preferring to sink rather than surrender to a Confederate ship.

Even when the vessel had sunk, it is said that the flag still floated above the waves for many hours.

Without a moment's rest, this iron fiend turned upon another Union vessel, and soon she, too, was a wreck. On went the Merrimac, attacking other vessels, until fortunately night came on and put a stop to this day's work; then she withdrew, to rest a while, chuckling no doubt over her day's doings, and planning all sorts of wickedness for the coming day. But to her great surprise, when the sun rose on the following morning, there stood not far away, a funny looking little vessel, dressed in fire-proof coat just like her own.

The Merrimac glared from all her port-holes at this funny looking affair, and for a time couldn't seem to get it through her stupid head what it was. It looked like an iron raft with a round iron box in the middle.

What in the world that box could be, and what could be inside the box were a wonder to the Merrimac.

"Does that little Yankee cheese-box on a raft think to fight with me?" said the Merrimac, puffed up with her yesterday's victories.

But the Merrimac did not know that that cheese-box could revolve on a big screw, and that it had within itself some terrible guns which could be aimed almost as true as a rifle.

Up came the little Monitor, much like a little hornet at a great bull. The Merrimac really laughed to see her coming. She did look so funny! But soon bang went one of the great two-hundred pound balls from that little cheese-box, shaking the Merrimac and denting in her iron sides as if she had been made of tin.

The Merrimac stopped laughing now, and went to work. Some one said that the whole affair made him think of the boy David with his little sling walking up to fight the giant Goliah. But you remember Goliah was the one to fall, and in this battle, too, the big Merrimac fell before the little "Cheese-box."

No matter what the Merrimac did, it seemed to harm the Monitor not one whit. The balls from the Merrimac rolled from her like raindrops from a duck's back.

Next, the Merrimac tried her game of running at her with that great iron beak; but only found herself all the more at the mercy of those great guns turning round and round in the cheese-box.

For four long hours this battle went on. At last the Merrimac quietly sailed away, not half understanding yet what this little raft was, and how it had been able to drive her away.

Cheer after cheer went up from the vessels lying about in the harbor; and there was no cause for further dread of the Confederate monster so long as the harbor was guarded by "The Yankee Cheese-box."

THE LAST BROADSIDE

Shall we give them a broadside, my boys, as she goes?
    Shall we send yet another to tell,
In iron-tongued words, to Columbia's foes,
    How bravely her sons say Farewell?

Ay! what though we sink 'neath the turbulent wave,
    'Tis with DUTY and RIGHT at the helm;
And over the form should the fierce waters rave,
    No tide can the spirit o'erwhelm!

For swift o'er the billows of Charon's dark stream
    We'll pass to the immortal shore,
Where the waters of life in brilliancy beam,
    And the pure float in peace evermore.

"Shall we give them a broadside once more, my brave men
    "Ay! Ay!" was the full, earnest cry;
"A broadside! A broadside! we'll give them again!
    Then for God and the Right nobly die!"

"Haste! Haste!"—for amid all that battling din
    Comes a gurgling sound fraught with fear,
As swift flowing waters pour rushingly in;
    Up! up! till her port-holes they near.

No blanching!—no faltering!—still fearless all seem;
    Each man firm to duty doth bide;

A flash! and a "broadside!" a shout! a careen!
　　And the Cumberland sinks 'neath the tide!

The "Star-Spangled Banner" still floating above!
　　As a beacon upon the dark wave!
Our Ensign of Glory, proud streaming in love,
　　O'er the tomb of the "Loyal and Brave!"

Bold hearts! mighty spirits! "tried gold" of our land!
　　A halo of glory your meed!
All honored, the noble-souled Cumberland band!
　　So true in Columbia's need!
　　　　　　　　　—Elizabeth T. P. Beach

BATTLE OF MILL SPRING—1862

In the battle of Mill Spring, the Confederates were put to flight by the Yankees.

One gentleman, whose slave had been sent with the Confederates into this battle, was questioning Sambo about what he had seen. Oftentimes these negroes were much brighter than their masters gave them credit for being.

"Well, Sambo, how long did it take you to march to the battle-field?"

" 'Bout four days, massa," was the reply.

"That was pretty good marching, I'm sure. How long did it take you to march back?"

" 'Bout two days, massa."

Only *two* days! why, that's strange. I shouldn't suppose soldiers after a long battle could march faster than before it."

"Dunno nuffin 'bout dat, massa; but I speck the music make de difference. You see, we marched there to the tune of Dixie; but we come back to tune of Fire! fire! fire! Run boys! Run!"

A BRAVE BOY AT FORT HENRY

Among the wounded in Fort Henry was a young Wisconsin boy, a prisoner, who had his arm shattered by a ball from one of the gunboats. He was taken into one of the cabins and a Confederate surgeon began to operate upon the injured limb. He had just bared the bone when a large shell came crashing through the hut. The little fellow kept on talking while the bone was being sawed, without showing the least fear. Soon another shot went by them.

"This is getting too hot for me," said the doctor; and taking the boy up in his arms he carried him into one of the bomb-proofs, where he finished the work.

"If you think this hot," replied the boy, "it will be a good deal too hot for you by and by."

"Ah!" said the doctor afterwards, "I should like to see that boy again. He was the bravest little fellow I ever saw."

TAKING OF DONELSON

Let us take a run over into Kentucky and Tennessee, and see what is going on there.

Columbus, at the western end of the Confederate lines, and Bowling Green at the eastern end, together with two strong forts, Donelson and Henry, made for the Confederates a centre that seemed almost too strong to be taken. The Confederates delighted to speak of this as their "Gibraltar," that is their stronghold.

But Grant, you all know who Grant was—was not to be frightened even by this. "It looked risky," he used to say; "but if we *can* get hold of these forts and these cities and break up this Confederate stronghold, think what a gain it will be!"

GEN. U. S. GRANT

66

When Grant had his plans all arranged, he gave them to his chief, and waited eagerly for permission to go on. After a long delay, permission came.

Fort Henry, being the weakest point, was to be attacked first.

"You, Commodore Foote, will take your men down the Tennessee River in gun-boats, and will pepper the fort from that point. When Fort Henry is settled, then comes Donelson."

Foote did pepper Fort Henry well; and in just one hour and five minutes the fort surrendered.

Six days later, Grant turned toward Fort Donelson. Spreading his forces out in a sort of half circle, he thus approached the fort. Grant made up his mind that the way to get hold of this fort would be to lay siege to it, rather than to try to bring about a battle.

But the Confederate officers knew only too well that they could not hold out against a siege, and so thought it best to give battle at once. The very next morning they came out and fell upon the right wing of Grant's army. Grant himself was down the river when the attack began; up he galloped to the scene of battle in a "double quick" run you may be sure.

"They have come out prepared to fight for several days, General," said one of the soldiers.

"Why do you think so?" asked Grant.

"Because they have their haversacks filled with rations," was the reply.

"Get me one of those haversacks," said Grant quickly.

One was brought. Grant examined it carefully, and saw that it was rationed for three days.

"This means retreat, retreat, boys," cried Grant. "Soldiers don't fill their haversacks like this unless they are planning to run away. Now then, one more sharp attack, and we'll finish the fight!"

The men, cheered by Grant's hopefulness, fell upon the enemy hot and heavy. With one grand push, the whole line made the attack. The fight grew hotter and hotter. Over the snow-covered ground everywhere ran streams of blood. Everywhere lay the dead and wounded. Darkness came on at last, thank God, and this awful slaughter was at an end.

The enemy were driven within their own lines. "One more hour of fighting," said Grant, "and the fort will be ours." Inside the fort two of the generals were packing up to get away before daylight. When morning dawned, General Buckner sent out to ask Grant on what terms he would be willing to accept their surrender.

"Unconditional surrender," said Grant, "are my only terms." By that he meant that they should surrender *wholly*, give up themselves and *all they had*, or he would fight them again and *make* them surrender.

General Buckner had little to say. He knew only too well that there was nothing to be done but surrender.

Grant's army marched in and took the fort.

On the same day the commander at Bowling Green saw fit to get his forces out of the way; and a few days later the commander at Columbus did the same. They knew very well that with both forts lost, the cities, too, would have to go. Even in the capital of the State, the governor packed his valuable papers and ran as if from a fire.

The great Confederate stronghold had fallen into the hands of Union troops. Great was the rejoicing in the Northern States. "Unconditional surrender!" came to be the "by-word" in every city and town; and Grant came to be called "Unconditional Surrender Grant."

This must be what his initials "U. S." mean, the people said in their joy. And to this day, no soldier hears of U. S. Grant without thinking of "Unconditional Surrender."

A PLUCKY BOY AT FORT DONELSON

A story is told of a little boy about eleven years old, whose father, a Union volunteer, had been taken prisoner some time before.

Having no mother, and no one to care for him, he made up his mind that he would go to fight his father's captors. So he smuggled himself on board of a boat laden with troops for the attack on Donelson. When the troops marched from Fort Henry, he joined the Seventy-eighth Ohio and trudged along with the rest. One of the officers questioned him and tried to turn him back, but he would not go.

On the field of battle he succeeded in getting a musket, and posting himself behind a tree fired at every head he saw above the enemy's breastwork. The Confederate sharp-shooters tried hard to drive him away, but he kept himself well hidden all the time.

At last a Confederate soldier on the outside of the breast-work took good aim at him, but the little fellow was too quick and brought him down with a shot from his musket. Knowing that the dead Confederate had a fine Minie rifle, the boy ran out, while the bullets were flying in all directions, and took from the soldier his rifle, cartouch and knapsack. Retreating in safety to his tree, he returned to the Seventy-eighth at night with all his prizes.

THE BATTLE OF SHILOH

After the fall of Donelson, the Confederates had gone down the river to Corinth. Here Beauregard and other commanders came with troops until there were forty thousand of them.

Grant had been closely following, and had halted at a place about twenty miles from Corinth. There had been some rumor that the Confederates were about to attack the Union soldiers, but this did not seem probable; and, hourly expecting more troops, the Union army was quietly sleeping, all unconscious of the terrible day to come. But all this time, the Confederates, forty thousand strong, were hidden in the forests all about, only waiting for daylight to begin their bloody work.

At daybreak, the Union soldiers of one camp were aroused by yells from the enemy. In a moment all was hurry and flurry. The news spread from camp to camp. Grant, who had the day before gone to a town near by for food for his army, heard the firing, and galloped to the battle grounds. Knowing that troops were coming to his aid, and could not be far away, he sent messengers post haste to hurry them up. If only they could hold out till help came, Grant was sure they yet might win.

The aim of the Confederates was to drive the Unionists down to the river, where, as there were no boats, they must either surrender or drown. Beauregard, the plucky little black-eyed general with the white hair, you remember, kept driving up and down his lines, crying, "Drive the Yankees into the river! drive the Yankees into the river!"

All day long this terrible battle raged; but when darkness fell, Beauregard gave orders for his men to rest till morning. A fortunate thing was this for the Union soldiers, for had he kept up the fight, he might indeed have driven the Yankees into the river.

Beauregard instead, however, withdrew to his tent, and there spent the night writing a full account of the brilliant victory so sure to come in the early morning.

But alas for his pretty plan! even while he was writing, the looked-for troops had arrived in Grant's camp. And when the morning sun arose, it looked upon the Union soldiers, fifty thousand strong, drawn up in battle array, ready to renew the fight.

It was plain enough what the end must be. But Beauregard was no coward. He made a brave show of fighting, although he knew he was being driven back with every charge. At noon, he ordered his forces to retreat, and soon the Union flag was waving over the "Battle-field of Shiloh."

THE OLD SERGEANT

BATTLE OF SHILOH
(PITTSBURG LANDING), TENN.

"Come a little nearer, Doctor,—thank you,—let me take the cup;
Draw your chair up,—draw it closer,—just another little sup!
Maybe you may think I'm better; but I'm pretty well used up,—
Doctor, you've done all you could do, but I'm just agoing up!

"Feel my pulse, sir, if you want to, but it ain't much use to try"—
"Never say that," said the surgeon, as he smothered down a sigh;
"It will never do, old comrade, for a soldier to say die!"
"What you say will make no difference, Doctor, when you come to die.

"Doctor, what has been the matter?" "You were very faint, they say;
You must try to get to sleep now." "Doctor, have I been away?"
"Not that anybody knows of!" "Doctor,— Doctor, please to stay!
There is something I must tell you, and you won't have long to stay!

"I have got my marching orders, and I'm ready now to go;
Doctor, did you say I fainted?—but it couldn't ha' been so.—
For as sure as I'm a Sergeant, and was wounded at Shiloh,
I've this very night been back there, on the old field of Shiloh!

THE OLD SERGEANT

"This is all that I remember: The last time the Lighter came,
 And the lights had all been lowered, and the noises much the same,
 He had not been gone five minutes before something called my name:
 'Orderly Sergeant—Robert Burton!'—just that way it called my name.

"And I wondered who could call me so distinctly and so slow,
 Knew it couldn't be the Lighter,—he could not have spoken so,—
 And I tried to answer, 'here, sir!' but I couldn't make it go;
 For I couldn't move a muscle, and I couldn't make it go;

"Then I thought: It's all a nightmare, all a humbug and a bore;
 Just another foolish grape-vine,*—and it won't come any more;
 But it came, sir, notwithstanding, just the same way as before
 'Orderly Sergeant—Robert Burton!'—even plainer than before.

"That is all that I remember, till a sudden burst of light,
 And I stood beside the river, where we stood that Sunday night,
 Waiting to be ferried over to the dark bluffs opposite,
 When the river was perdition and all hell was opposite!

"And the same old palpitation came again in all its power,
 And I heard a bugle sounding as from some celestial tower;
 And the same mysterious voice said: 'It is the eleventh hour!
 Orderly Sergeant—Robert Burton—it is the eleventh hour!'

"Doctor Austin! what day is this?" "It is Wednesday night, you know."
"Yes,—to-morrow will be New Year's, and a right good time below!
"What time is it, Doctor Austin?" "Nearly twelve." "Then don't you go!
Can it be that all this happened—all this—not an hour ago!

"There was where the gunboats opened on the dark, rebellious host;
 And where Webster semicircled his last guns upon the coast;
 There were still the two log-houses, just the same,
        or else their ghost,—
 And the same old transport came and took me over,—or its ghost!

* Canard.

75

"And the old field lay before me all deserted far and wide;
  There was where they fell on Prentiss,—there McClernand
      met the tide;

There was where stern Sherman rallied, and where Hurlbut's
      heroes died,—
Lower down, where Wallace charged them, and kept charging
      till he died.

"There was where Lew Wallace showed them he was of the canny kin,
  There was where old Nelson thundered, and where Rosseau waded in;
  There McCook sent 'em to breakfast, and we all began to win,—
  There was where the grape-shot took me, just as we began to win.

"Now, a shroud of snow and silence over everything was spread;
  And but for this old blue mantle, and the old hat on my head,
  I should not have even doubted, to this moment I was dead,—
  For my footsteps were as silent as the snow upon the dead!

"Death and silence!—Death and silence all round me as I sped!
  And behold, a mighty tower, as if builded to the dead.
  To the heaven of the heavens lifted up its mighty head,
  Till the Stars and Stripes of heaven all seemed waving from its head!

"Round and mighty-based it towered,— up into the infinite,—
  And I knew no mortal mason could have built a shaft so bright,
  For it shone like solid sunshine; and a winding-stair of light
  Wound around it and around it till it wound clear out of sight!

"And, behold, as I approached it, with a wrapt and dazzled stare,—
  Thinking that I saw old comrades just ascending the great stair,
  Suddenly the solemn challenge broke of—'Halt, and who goes there?'
  'I'm a friend,' I said 'if you are.' 'Then advance, sir, to the stair!'

"I advanced! That sentry, Doctor, was Elijah Ballantyne!—
  First of all to fall on Monday, after we had formed the line!—
  'Welcome, my old Sergeant, welcome! Welcome by that countersign!'
  And he pointed to the scar there, under this old cloak of mine!

THE OLD SERGEANT

"As he grasped my hand, I shuddered, thinking only of the grave;
  But he smiled and pointed upward with a bright and bloodless glaive;

'That's the way, sir, to head-quarters.' 'What head-quarters?'
        'Of the brave.'
'But the great tower?' 'That,' he answered, 'is the way, sir, of the brave!'

"Then a sudden shame came o'er me, at his uniform of light;
  At my own so old and tattered, and at his so new and bright:
  'Ah!' said he, 'you have forgotten the new uniform to-night,—
  Hurry back, for you must be here just at twelve o'clock to-night!'

"And the next thing I remember, you were sitting there, and I—
  Doctor, did you hear a footstep? Hark!—God bless you all! Good-by!
  Doctor, please to give my musket and my knapsack, when I die,
  To my son—my son that's coming,—he won't get here till I die!

"Tell him his old father blessed him as he never did before,—
  And to carry that old musket"—Hark! a knock is at the door!—
  "Till the Union"—See it opens! "Father! Father! speak once more!"
  "Bless you!" gasped the old, gray Sergeant, and he lay and said no more!

                                        —FORCEYTHE WILSON.

77

BROTHER AGAINST BROTHER

It often happened in the "civil war," that one in a family would fight on the Union side, and another on the Confederate side—each one fighting on the side which to him seemed right.

In Kentucky, where the people were so divided in their opinions of the war, that one hardly could tell whether to call Kentucky a Union State or a Confederate State, it often happened that own brothers would meet fighting face to face in battle.

At the battle of Shiloh, during the hottest of the strife, it happened that two of these Kentucky regiments met and fought each other with the fury and hatred which usually marks civil warfare. One of the Union soldiers happened to wound and take prisoner his own brother; and after handing him to the rear, began firing at a man near a tree. "Hold, Bill," shouted his captured brother, "don't shoot there any more! That's father!"

QUAKER GUNS

But it is about time to hear something from that "Army of the Potomac." You remember I told you a few pages back that this was a large, fresh army, sent from the North. The people expected great things of this army, and were very impatient to see them go to work.

For a long time the enemy had been holding that railroad junction that you heard of not long ago, so that there was no way of getting to Richmond, the capital of the Confederacy. I should not have said there was *no* way of getting to this city—of course there were ways; but here was this railroad running straight to the city, carrying the Confederates food and clothing every day, and so helping to keep them able to fight on and on against their country. "If only this capital could be taken, the war might be as good as ended," every one said. In that city were stored food and blankets, guns and powder—everything that their army could need. "Why *doesn't* McClellan march the Army of the Potomac to take it!" everybody cried.

At last McClellan *did* move. He started his army on to this junction, this stronghold of the Southerners. The troops marched on, expecting, I presume, a terrible fight; but imagine their surprise when on reaching there they found it empty. Every Confederate had fled. More than that, on examining their camp they found that the guns, those terrible guns, which had been so long frightening back the Union Army, were just nothing in the world but big logs, their ends cut out to look like cannon-mouths, and painted black! One of them, even, was only an old stove-pipe! I wonder which this army felt the most—ashamed, or amused, or angry—that all these weeks they had been trembling before these Quaker guns!

Later, McClellan marched his forces upon York-town. Here they kept up a siege for more than a month. But one morning it was found that the enemy had run away in the night in the same way they had run away before. This time, too, they left nothing to pay the Union Army for their long work, except some old guns. This Confederate, General Johnston, had a way of retreating in this clever way; and came to be named in time, the "successful retreater."

DARK DAYS

A long, long time of defeats for the Union army followed. The Confederates were getting themselves together at Richmond, their capital. They knew that was their stronghold and supposed of course the Union army knew it, too, and would before many days bear down upon them.

GEN. R. E. LEE

Down to the banks of the Chicka-hominy went our "Army of the Potomac." This river was a sluggish, muddy stream, with swamps on every side. The army was set to work digging trenches, and throwing up banks of earth to defend them from the Confederate force in Richmond. This was a sad, sad time. In this damp, unhealthy spot, our soldiers worked on day and night. Unused to the climate, the men began to die as if seized with a plague. Hundreds and hundreds of them sank beneath the poison of the place, and every day our "Army of the Potomac" grew smaller and smaller.

Again McClellan stood still. Johnston, the "successful retreater," not wishing to retreat this time, came out from the city and attacked McClellan himself at *Fair Oaks*. Fortune favored our side in the battle, and Johnston was *made* to retreat this time into the city.

Johnston was wounded in this battle; and so, unfitted for service, he was obliged to give up his command. Robert Lee became the Confederate commander in his place. McClellan still hesitated to push forward and his men were dying off in hundreds.

Stonewall Jackson now arrived at Richmond and joined his forces with those of Lee's.

McClellan still waited, until the enemy again came out and, by attacking him, forced him to act. Now began a series of battles called the "Seven Days' Battles." Every day for a week the two armies engaged in battle, and every day McClellan ordered "retreat, retreat." On the seventh day the Union forces, from a high ridge of land, poured down their fire with such vigor and such success that the enemy, powerful as they were, were driven back broken and confused, having lost greatly in dead and wounded. Even now it is a mystery, explained one way by some, another way by others that McClellan, brave and well-trained as he was should have held his forces back as he did week after week, apparently doing nothing.

Certainly he had some reason for his action (or lack of action) whatever it was. Perhaps some soldier who was in the war can tell you all about it. You and I could hardly form a just opinion regarding it. So, for now, let us go on and read about a battle between McClellan and the brave southern general—Lee.

THE SONG OF THE CAMPS

Far away in the piny woods,
    Where the dews fall heavy and damp,
A soldier sat by the smouldering fire
    And sang the song of the camp.

"It is not to be weary and worn,
    It is not to feel hunger and thirst,
It is not the forced march, nor the terrible fight,
    That seems to the soldier the worst;

"But to sit through the comfortless hours,—
    The lonely, dull hours that will come—
With his head in his hands, and his eyes on the fire,
    And his thoughts on visions of home;

"To wonder how fares it with those
    Who mingled so late with his life,—
Is it well with my little children three?
    Is it well with my sickly wife?
                —J. R. M.

LEE IS KEPT FROM ENTERING PENNSYLVANIA

Having so little success in trying to raise troops in Maryland, Lee next decided to go over into the State of Pennsylvania. There he proposed to have Stonewall Jackson join his army, and together they would go on to the very city of New York.

GEN. BURNSIDE

Now it happened, as Lee's army left Frederick on their march through Pennsylvania, some one of his generals accidentally dropped a paper in the streets, upon which was written the one thing of all others which Lee would not for the world have had the Unionists find out. And that was just what General Lee had planned to do; just the route he intended to take; just how he was going to divide his army; and just where he intended to bring them together for battle.

McClellan at once set out in hot haste to overtake this army. On the 16th of September, both armies lay down to sleep in the beautiful, fertile valley of Antietam, knowing that with the rising of the sun must come one of the hottest contested battles of the war.

It was a long bloody battle. Both sides lost, in killed and wounded, large numbers; but neither side could be said to have won the day. It was one of those terrible battles, in which both sides merely held their places, seeming, with all the bloodshed, to gain nothing. The next morning was to have seen the battle renewed; but McClellan, seized again with his overcautiousness, waited and waited. The next day, Lee escaped over the Potomac. His plans were all broken up by this battle with its terrible losses, and it seemed at the time as if McClellan might, if he had made one bold stroke, have done a great deal more even than that.

But McClellan now again waited and waited, although he had been ordered by Lincoln to march against the enemy. At last, Lincoln ordered that the command be taken from him, and given to General Burnside.

Lee was now encamped at Fredricksburg. Burnside at once marched against him, and attempted to take the city from him. A hot battle followed, but at night Lee was still in the city, and the Union army had again lost hundreds of men.

And now the army was led back to the old camps. There the soldiers built mud huts; and, sick and wounded, their courage all gone, they settled down for the winter.

This campaign in Virginia had been a wretched failure for the Union army.

THE BATTLE OF ANTIETAM

BARBARA FRIETCHIE

(CONCERT READING)

Up from the meadows rich with corn,
Clear in the cool September morn,

The cluster'd spires of Frederick stand,
Green-wall'd by the hills of Maryland.

Round about them orchards sweep,
Apple and peach-tree fruited deep,

Fair as a garden of the Lord,
To the eyes of the famish'd rebel horde,

On that pleasant morn of the early Fall,
When Lee march'd over the mountain wall,

Over the mountains winding down,
Horse and foot, into Frederick town.

Forty flags with their silver stars,
Forty flags with their crimson bars,

Flapp'd in the morning wind: the sun
Of noon look'd down, and saw not one.

Up rose old Barbara Frietchie then,

BARBARA FRIETCHIE

Bow'd with her fourscore years and ten;

Bravest of all in Frederick town,
She took up the flag the men haul'd down,

In her attic window the staff she set,
To show that one heart was loyal yet.

Up the street came the rebel tread,
Stonewall Jackson riding ahead.

Under his slouch'd hat, left and right,
He glanced; the old flag met his sight:

"Halt!"—the dust-brown ranks stood fast.
"Fire!"—out blazed the rifle-blast.

It shivered the window, pane and sash;
It rent the banner with seam and gash.

Quick as it fell from the broken staff
Dame Barbara snatched the silken scarf.

She leaned far out on the window-sill,
And shook it forth with a royal will.

"Shoot, if you must, this old gray head,
But spare your country's flag," she said.

A shade of sadness, a blush of shame
Over the face of the leader came;

"Who touches a hair of yon gray head,
Dies like a dog! March on!" he said.

All day long through Frederick street
Sounded the tread of marching feet;

All day long that free flag tossed
Over the heads of the rebel host.

Barbara Frietchie's work is o'er,
And the rebel rides on his raids no more.

BARBARA FRIETCHIE

THE VIRGINIA ARMY

Now Gen. Pope was ordered to take command of an army of about 50,000, called the "Virginia Army." Very soon it was plain to see that Lee was planning to attack Washington. It was bad enough that our army had not succeeded in taking the Confederate capital; but to have them take Washington!—"No, indeed," said Gen. Pope. "No, indeed," echoed the soldiers.

The two armies met at Cedar Mountain. Here followed one of the most ghastly, most bloody battles of the whole war. Both sides lost great numbers of men, and neither side can be said to have gained much over the other.

Soon more battles were fought, among them another at Bull Run. Bull Run seemed an unlucky place for the Unionists. A second time they were defeated there, but this time there was no shameful running away. At last, Pope's army, called the "Army of Virginia," was ordered to Washington. They were as broken-spirited as McClellan's army had been.

It seemed as if the Fates were against the Union forces. Gen. Pope had been a hero in the West, fighting fiercely, full of hope and daring, a terror to the enemy. Now all seemed changed. Every attack had been a failure.

Now the two armies, the "Army of the Potomac" and the "Army of Virginia" were united—what there was left of them—and Gen. McClellan was again put in command.

Gen. McClellan had been a great favorite among his men, and when he was again put in command, it is said his men received him with shouts of joy; cheers for "Little Mac," as they called him, filled the air.

Gen. Lee meantime was on his way northward. First, he meant to stir up Maryland, and find men there to join his army. Maryland, you remember, had not seceded. Still, Lee knew there were many there who in heart were "secessionists."

So into that State he marched to the old southern tune, "Maryland, My Maryland." It was a beautiful old song, and was often played in the Confederate lines, as "Rally Round the Flag, Boys" was played in our lines.

Some way the Maryland people could not be aroused, not even by Lee. They refused to have anything whatever to do with the war. I think Lee's army at this time would hardly have inspired any one with a very great desire to join it. Successful though they had been, they were a wretched looking company. Ragged, hungry, hatless and coatless, often shoeless. "Stonewall Jackson" himself, it is said, was so shabby and worn, that he looked quite as bad as his troops.

Such brave men as these were, never shrinking from any hardship, ready to do and to die, doesn't it seem a pity they were fighting in such a wretched cause—fighting to save a government, which as they had said, should have the buying and selling of slaves as the corner-stone?

CAPTURE OF
NEW ORLEANS

New Orleans, situated at the mouth of the Mississippi, was held by the Confederates. Because it is at the mouth of this great river, you can easily see it was necessary that the Unionists should have it, in order that they might be free to go up and down this great river whenever they chose.

Said Gen. Butler in his usual direct way, "New Orleans should be in our hands, New Orleans can be taken, and I can take it." There were many reasons why it seemed a doubtful place to attack, but Butler usually succeeded in whatever he set out to do; and, as his men often said, could make his hearers believe "the moon was made of green cheese" if he chose.

Soon Butler was on his way to New Orleans. He was very careful to keep his purpose hidden.

On reaching "Ship Island," a low sandy island off the coast of Mississippi, he found it covered all over with little white tents. This was the camp of Gen. Phelps, who, with 6,000 soldiers, was eagerly awaiting Butler's coming.

Here Butler was joined by Admiral Farragut, one of the most remarkable naval officers America ever had. Together these two men planned to take New Orleans. Now, this city is a Mississippi sea-port; but it is situated around the corner, up the river a few miles, and was fortified strongly at every point. One could not even enter the river without passing two forts, and then there were many more dangerous points farther on. The only way to get *to* the city even, was either to bombard these forts and make them surrender, or else pass quietly by, letting the forts turn their great guns upon the vessels as they passed along. Neither the one, nor the other was a simple thing to do.

But danger or no danger, both Butler and Farragut were determined to reach that city.

Farragut had forty-eight vessels in all, and they carried three hundred and ten great guns.

Some of the vessels were covered over with a heavy network of iron chains to protect them from the balls from the forts. Their hulks were painted a dark, dull color, so that they could hardly be seen as they lay in the dull, muddy colored river. Then great trees were laced on the vessels' sides; so covering them up, and making them look so much like bits of the forests on the river banks, that, as they stole up the river in the dark night, the soldiers in the forts should not notice them until they were right upon them.

At last all was ready; and at three o'clock in the morning, this strange-looking fleet entered the Mississippi.

The first trouble that met them was a fire boat. This was a great raft, piled up with wood which had been soaked with oil. This was to be pushed up close to some Union vessel, to set it on fire. Of course such a fire as that oiled wood would make, would very soon catch the vessel before anything could be done to save her. And if this pile of pitch and oil were to get in among the tree-covered vessels, there would be a terrible scene!

"A boat! a boat!" cried the soldiers. "Volunteers to tow away this fire raft." "I" and "I!" and "I!" answered brave men from Farragut's fleet. A boat was lowered and rowed swiftly up to this blazing pile. Grappling irons were thrown and caught fast among the timbers, and away she was towed out of reach of the Union vessels. All by herself, on the water's edge she burned and snapped and crackled, doing no harm, only making of herself a most beautiful bonfire.

Fort Jackson was attacked first. Now followed a fierce siege. For three days the gun boats and the fort kept up the fire. Cannonball and bombshell! Smoke and flash! Roar upon roar, till it seemed as if the very earth did quake! Fish, killed by the shock, floated dead upon the river. Windows thirty miles away were broken in pieces, shaken by the jarring thunder.

A little farther up the river it was found that iron cables had been drawn across, linking together a chain of hulks, and so making passage beyond them almost impossible But nothing seemed impossible to Farragut's men.

These cables *must* be broken. That seemed the only thought. And so again under cover of darkness, two gun-boats were sent to break the cable. With hammer and chisel they worked away, and lo! the cable parted, and down the stream the hulks floated, leaving the passage free.

Up the river steamed the brave fleet, past the forts which threw out a rain of fire and shot upon them, straight through a fleet of confederate gun-boats, sent from New Orleans to prevent their approach to the city. And at last the Union fleet steamed up to the very wharves of the city, demanding its surrender. The people stood aghast! They had believed it impossible to reach their city. All the time the bombarding of the forts had been going on, these people had laughed and joked about it, never once thinking that Farragut could pass the forts, the fire-boats, the cables! But here he was at daybreak, at their very doors!

The people were panic stricken. What should they do? Where should they go? "Burn the city! Burn the city!" cried the men. "Yes, burn the city, and we will help you! The Yankees shall not have our homes!" cried the women.

But now news came that Butler, too, had passed the forts safely and was rapidly approaching by land. This was the last blow; and the people settled down to their fate with sullen faces, and with hearts full of hatred and revenge.

In marched Butler with flags flying, his bands filling the air with strains of Union music. Can you blame these New Orleans men and women that they hated these Union soldiers?

How the people glared at them! how they muttered and growled! The women, it is said, were more bitter than the men. They were like lionesses aroused to battle. They would not pass a Union soldier on the street. They would go out into the middle of the street rather than to meet one of the officers. The Union officers were insulted on every hand.

Gen. Butler realized how bitter a trial the taking of their city was to them, as we all do. But he could not and would not allow the Union officers, much more the Union flag, to be insulted. He at once took military command of the city, hoisted the "Stars and Stripes" and forced the people to pay, at least, outward respect to his soldiers.

Did you ever read "Uncle Tom's Cabin?" I don't suppose you have—it is too old for you yet—but perhaps you have seen it played. You remember little Eva, the little girl, who was so good to the slaves. You remember Old Uncle Tom, whose good old heart was nearly broken when he thought he must go away from his "little missus," as he always called the little Eva. And do you remember Eliza, the slave woman with the little baby, who was hunted through the forests and across the rivers, the wicked old slave-owner and his cruel pack of hounds at her heels?

Before the war broke out, Gen. Butler read this story of "Uncle Tom's Cabin;" but didn't approve of it at all. He didn't believe any such cruelty was to be found in the South. But when he left New Orleans, where he lived for nearly a year, he said, "Mrs. Stowe has told the truth in her book. I have seen with my own eyes and have heard with my own ears treatment of slaves here in the South a thousand times worse than anything that Mrs. Stowe has put into 'Uncle Tom's Cabin even.'"

SECESSION WOMEN

Of course, all the women in the United States were not Unionists. You have already heard how the Southern women treated the Union officers whenever they met them on the streets. Do you remember how angry the New Orleans women were when Butler came? But these Southern women, who believed that their side was right, and that the Unionists were but thieves and robbers, were not content with being merely angry. They worked for their soldiers just as the Northern women worked for theirs.

There are some funny stories told of ways in which these bright-witted women used to plan to carry help to the Confederate soldiers.

It was the fashion then for ladies to wear very large hoops; and these ladies soon found it very convenient to fasten packages and letters to the wires of these hoops, and so carry them to the soldiers.

One lady was found to have on a quilted skirt which weighed fifty pounds. What do you suppose she had hidden in this wonderful skirt? You may be sure it was something for the soldiers. It was filled in all among the quiltings with sewing silk for the doctors in the army to use for sewing up wounds, and a medicine, called quinine, which is believed to be very good for fever and chills.

All trunks and boxes and packages that went out from Washington on the train were carefully searched; and sometimes, I fancy, very strange things were found in them.

One story is told of a little red, wooden trunk, marked Mary Berkitt, Wheeling, Virginia. It was a very innocent looking little trunk, looking as if it might belong to some old lady perhaps. But the officers had learned from experience that the most innocent looking people and the most innocent trunks sometimes held the greatest secrets. So Old Lady Mary's trunk was looked into. On the top, lay some clothing, very neatly packed, and under these some dresses.

"Never mind that trunk," said an officer; "there's nothing under there but the old lady's caps."

"Can't be too sure," answered the officer in charge, still pulling out the clothing. Down at the very bottom of the trunk, the caps were found indeed. Hundreds and hundreds of them—more than the old lads could ever wear in a whole lifetime, you will think. Yes, indeed; but you see, boys, they happened to be percussion-caps; and the officer, thinking them more useful for him than for her, emptied them all out, and I fear Mary never saw her trunk again.

THE MOCK FUNERAL

All sorts of ways were invented to carry help across from Maryland to the Confederate states; and you may be sure the officers had to keep their eyes wide open day and night.

One day, on a train, as innocent a looking thing as a lunch basket with a sandwich and a doughnut plainly in sight, was found to be filled with bright brass buttons, on their way to ornament the Confederate soldiers' coats.

But one of the strangest plots for carrying help was by means of funeral processions. One day a very sober looking procession started out from Baltimore over the Long Bridge, into Virginia.

Everything appeared all right. There was the hearse with the coffin within; then came the carriages, their curtains closely drawn to hide the mourners from the people on the streets; the drivers all looked solemn as owls, and to all appearances, it was a very respectable looking funeral procession.

The first sentry at the Bridge, feeling that a funeral procession, of all things, should be allowed to go on its sad way without being interfered with, let it pass—although, as he said afterwards, it *did* flash across his mind that even this might be but another Confederate scheme.

The next sentry on the route, was not so easily fooled. Perhaps he had learned that even funeral processions in those times were suspicious. Stepping forward as the hearse approached, he called "Halt!"

Instantly he caught a look upon the driver's face that told him that something was wrong.

"Open the hearse!" demanded the sentry. The hearse was opened and the coffin dragged out. But by this time, the mourners in the carriages had learned that their plot was discovered; and when the sentry turned to look at them, they were scrambling out of their carriages, and running back to the city just as fast as ever they could go.

On opening the coffin, it was found packed full of muskets, which at that time would have been very acceptable to the Confederate army.

One of the ways the Confederates in Maryland had of getting messages across the river, was by means of kites and balloons. When kites were used, they were made of oiled silk, that the rain might not spoil them, nor the water, should they chance to fall into the river. The bobs of the kites were made of letters and newspapers, fastened on just as you boys fasten the bobs to your kites to-day.

When the wind was in the right direction, these kites were sent up, their strings cut, and across the river they would fly, falling somewhere on the Virginia shore. Some one was always on the watch for these kites; and when the wind turned, back would come the kite laden with letters and papers from the South.

AFFAIRS IN THE WEST

While all these defeats and losses were going on, out in the far West our soldiers were winning laurels for themselves.

Gen. Bragg, a Confederate officer, had cut round behind a part of our army, and had got his forces well into Kentucky. For six weeks this army marched about from place to place, destroying everything and pretty nearly everybody that came in its way.

At last he began collecting his forces with a view to swooping down upon St. Louis. The people of this city were frightened indeed. A panic would surely have followed but for Gen. Lew Wallace. He at once took charge of everything; called for troops, built defences, and, indeed, so quickly did he work, that by the time one of Bragg's divisions reached there, everything was ready for them. The advancing general saw they were ready—indeed, too ready, he thought; so when darkness fell, he turned his troops and marched back to join Gen. Bragg.

I want you to remember this Gen. Lew Wallace; for you are sure to hear of him by and by as you grow older, not so much as a soldier, but as an author.

Haven't you seen your mamma or papa reading a book called "Ben Hur?" Or haven't you heard them speak of it? It is a wonderful book, and I fancy Gen. Lew Wallace and his beautiful story will be remembered long after the bugles of this war are half forgotten. Some day when you are older you will read "Ben Hur," and then you will remember that the writer of that book was a general in this Civil War, about which you read when you were little boys and girls.

Bragg had all this time been loading himself with riches in Kentucky. He had fitted out his army with shoes and clothing, had filled his wagons with food, and had seized the splendid Kentucky horses for his cavalry; more than this, he had sent car-load after car-load of these things to the South.

Gen. Buell went against Bragg, but, as usual, fortune seemed to smile on the Confederate side. Gen. Rosecrans then went against a division of Bragg's army. A terrible battle, lasting all one day, took place at Corinth. During the night the Union troops, with their contraband helpers, threw up new defences and strengthened the old one. Early the next morning, with a terrible yell, called in this war the "rebel yell," the Confederates charged upon the Union ranks.

At first the Unionists fell back; but gathering themselves up, they closed round the enemy. Now the field was a scene of terrible slaughter. The Confederates fled, the Unionists at their heels, pouring in their shot upon them as they ran. At last the Unionists had won a victory.

Now Rosecrans was sent to take charge of the "Army of the Cumberland," as this western army was called.

Bragg had settled down at a place called Murfreesboro', and Jefferson Davis had come on to visit him. A grand, good time Bragg and the men were having; giving parties, attending balls, and giving themselves up generally to a good time.

But all this time the wise Rosecrans was laying in a store of provisions, and getting himself ready for a long fight if necessary.

An attack came. A terrible attack it was, too. A hot battle; and much bravery was shown on both sides.

Up and down rode Rosecrans, crying, "We must win this battle, boys!" no matter what he saw or what he heard. For two long days this battle raged, and at last the Confederates gave way, and in a few hours Bragg marched away, bag and baggage, leaving the field to the Union soldiers.

SHARP-SHOOTERS

Do you remember the sharp-shooters who came into Washington's camp during the Revolution? Do you remember how they used to amuse themselves while they were encamped outside of Boston, by shooting at targets just for the practice?

Well, there were sharp-shooters in the Civil War, too, both among the Unionists and among the Confederates. Their business was to be always on the watch when the armies were encamped near each other; and, if one of the enemy showed himself anywhere in sight, to shoot at him.

John D. Champlain, who has lately written a history of this war for young folks, tells this story of sharp-shooting:

"One of the most skilful of the Confederate marksmen was a large negro, who used to perch himself in a tree and lie there all day, firing whenever he saw a chance for a good shot. He had in this way killed several Union soldiers, and the sharp-shooters had watched a long time for him. At last the Union trenches, which were gradually being dug nearer and nearer, reached a place only about twenty rods from the tree. One morning the darky came out early and took his accustomed place in the tree. The sharp-shooters might have easily killed him as he came out, but they did not want to frighten others who were coming. He was followed soon by several Confederate pickets, on whom the men fired, killing some and driving the others back. The darky, of course, was now "in a fix", or, in other words, was "up a tree," for he could not get back without running the risk of being shot.

"I say, big nigger," called out one of the Union marksmen from the trenches, "you'd better come down from there."

"What for?" he asked.

"I want you as a prisoner."

"Not as this chile knows of," he answered.

"All right. Just as you say," called out the marksman.

In about an hour Mr. Darkey, hearing nothing from in front of his tree, concluded that it was safe to take just one peep; so he poked his head out far enough to get a look at the Union lines. But the sharp-shooter had not taken his eye from the tree for an instant, and no sooner did the head appear than he pulled the trigger of his rifle. A little puff of blue smoke—a flash—the whiz of a bullet—and down came the negro to the ground shot through the head.

STEALING POTATOES

The soldiers often got tired enough of these hard, dry biscuits and the salt meat, and would go out, in the night time, on stealing expeditions. The farmers used to complain bitterly of the soldiers; for they not only would steal everything they could find, but they would trample down the growing vegetables wherever they went.

One day, a good natured old farmer, whose potato fields had been nearly ruined by these half-starved soldiers, came into the camp hoping to find some trace of the thieves. While strolling around among the tents, he saw one of the boys serving up a dish of fine potatoes, which he thought looked very much like his own.

"Have fine potatoes here, I see," he said, halting before the tent.

"Splendid."

"Where do you get them?"

"Draw them."

"Does the government furnish potatoes for rations?"

"Nary tater."

"But I thought you said you drew them."

"Did. We just do that thing."

"But how—if they are not included in your rations?"

"Easiest thing in the world. Won't you take some with us?"

"Thank you. But you will oblige me if you will tell me how you draw your potatoes."

"Nothing easier. Draw 'em by the tops, mostly; sometimes with a hoe, if there's one left in the field."

"Ha! yes! I understand. Well, now, see here. If you won't draw any more of my potatoes, I'll bring you a basketful every morning and draw 'em myself."

"Now will you? Good for you, old fellow!"

And three cheers and a tiger were given for the farmer, who had the pleasure in future of drawing his own potatoes.

JOE PARSONS

At one of the hospitals, was a boy of twenty, who had been shot in the eyes. He used to enjoy sitting by the window, his eyes bandaged, and singing: "O, I'm a sojer boy!"

"What's your name, my boy?" asked a visitor.

"Joe Parsons, sir?"

"What is the matter with you?"

"Blind, sir, blind as a bat; shot at Antietam.

"But it might ha' been worse," he said. "I'm thankful I'm alive, sir."

"You see, I was hit, yer see, and it knocked me down. I lay there all night, and in the morning the fight began again. I could stand the pain, but the balls were flyin' all round, and I wanted to get away. At last I heard a groan beyond me."

"Hallo," said I. "Hallo, yourself," said he.

"Who are you?" said I. "A Gray Jacket?"

"Yes," said he; "and you're a Blue Jacket."

"My leg is broken," said he.

"Can you see?" said I.

"Yes."

"Well, I can't; but, I can walk. Now if you'll do the seeing, I'll do the walking and get us both away from here."

"All right; agreed."

"So that's the way we saved ourselves. And now I'm getting along pretty well."

"But my poor boy," said the visitor, "you will never see again."

"Yes I know that, but—'I'm a bold, bold sojer boy.' "

"A bold, bold sojer boy"—and the visitor passed on, leaving Joe singing as merry as a lark.

THE HOME SIDE OF THE WAR PICTURE

It would not be fair at all to the women and children of these times, neither do I think it would be a true story of the war if I were to tell you of nothing but the battles. Battles are terrible enough; or if you think so, grand enough, and brave enough. But you must not think that the whole of war is carried on in the battle-field.

Suppose, little boy and little girl, there were a war going on in our country to-day. Suppose *your* father were to go as a soldier to this war. He might look very fine as he marched away in his blue coat, with its gilt braid and its brass buttons. You might be very proud of him, as no doubt you would be; but do you think that would be all, just your seeing him look handsome and brave, and your feeling proud of him?

I am afraid after he had gone and the house was so quiet, and mamma looked so pale and white, and every day when the newspaper came you hardly dared read it for fear you would learn that your papa had been shot dead, or that he had been put into the black prisons—I am afraid you would come to think that

114

there was something more to war than plumes and brass buttons.

And suppose, by and by, you should hear that your papa was starving, that his shoes and stockings were all worn out, and that his feet were lame and sore from marching the hot, rough roads, and that he was sick and dying!

Suppose as the long weeks went on, mamma should have to go out to find some work to earn money to feed you and your little brothers and sisters—would war seem then a beautiful thing, do you think?

But this is what always does come into the homes when the papas and the big brothers go to the battle field. Mamma's heart grows very heavy, I fear; and the little children, too, begin to learn that war is a sad, sad thing.

But in this civil war of ours, I must tell you how brave these mothers and children were. How generous they were and how willing to work.

The rich sent money and food for the soldiers most freely; but the clothes, the stockings,—these things came usually from the poor who had no money to give. Everywhere societies were formed, called "Soldiers' Relief Societies." The rich would bring to these societies money and cloth and yarn, and the poor people who had nothing to give, would take the cloth and the yarn home to make up into clothes and stockings for the soldiers. In among these wretched battles, I must tell you a story now and then about these good women and children.

LILLIE'S FIVE-DOLLAR GOLD PIECE

A lady at the head of one of these relief societies tells this story:

A little girl not nine years old, with sweet and timid grace, came into the rooms, and laying a five-dollar gold piece on our desk, half frightened, told us its history. "My uncle gave me that before the war, and I was going to keep it always; but he's got killed in the army, and mother says now I may give it to the soldiers if I want to—and I'd like to do so. I don't suppose it will buy much for them, will it?" We led the child to the store-room, and showed her how valuable her gift was, by pointing out what it would buy—so many cans of milk, or so many bottles of ale, or pounds of tea, or codfish, etc. Her face brightened with pleasure. But when we explained to her that her five-dollar gold piece was equal to seven dollars and a half in greenbacks, and told her how much comfort we could carry into a hospital, with the stores that sum would buy, she fairly danced with joy.

"Oh, it will do lots of good, won't it?" And folding her hands before her, she begged, in her charmingly modest way, "Please tell me something that you've seen in the hospitals?"

We told her a few little stories—taking care to tell this little child nothing of the horrors of hospital life and death.

Then with tears in her eyes, she said, "Lady, I am going to save every single penny I have for the soldiers; and I'm going to ask all the little girls I know to save theirs, too." Dear Little Lillie! Who can tell what a world of good her five-dollar gold piece with all her love behind it, did for some poor soldier.

WHAT SOME POOR PEOPLE DID FOR THE SOLDIERS

Up among the mountains, in a farming district, lived a mother and her daughters. They were very poor—too poor by far to buy anything to send the soldiers.

Twelve miles away, over the mountain, was a town in which was one of these "Soldiers' Relief Societies."

"Let us go over the mountain, daughters," said the old mother, "and bring home some work to do for the soldiers. We have no money to give, but, we can find a little time, I am sure, to work for them."

"Yes, indeed," said the daughters; "we can get up earlier and milk the cows, and feed the chickens and the pigs; we can hurry a little with our planting and all the rest of the farm-work, and so make time to sew and knit for the soldiers."

Now, when you think that these three women had all the work to do both in the house and on the farm, and that their farm was all the means of gaining food that they had, you can see that they had quite as much to do as they had time or strength for without taking work home. Nevertheless every two weeks one of these three women used to ride into the village for work. Poorly clad, looking always as if very little of the good things of life had ever come to them, dusty and tired from their long ride, back and forth they came with their little offerings of work.

"I presume you have some dear one in the army," said one of the officers to these women one day.

"No," said they; "none now; our only brother was killed at the Battle of Ball's Bluff. But for his sake, and for our country's sake, we do all we can for the soldiers."

In another little village, lived a widow and her one little girl. Papa had left them to join the army. Mamma worked and the little girl worked for food and clothes till papa should come back to them. But one day the news came that he could never come to them again—he had fallen in the battle of Fair Oaks. They worked on still; and although they earned so little, they saved enough money, and found enough time, to make a quilt for the hospital, a pair of socks and a shirt. All winter long, these two, mother and child, worked through the long evenings to make these. "Papa died in the hospital," the little girl used to say; "and perhaps he needed these things. Perhaps some other little girl made the quilt that kept him warm, so we will make this one to keep some other good soldier warm."

Many a little girl went without candy in these days, many a little boy went without toys, that they might save their money for the soldiers.

One little girl, only five years old, knit a pair of stockings to send to the soldiers. Such a little girl! I suspect her mamma had now and then to take a stitch for her on them. But nevertheless the little girl's love was in them from top to toe. On them she pinned a little note, saying, "These socks was nit by a little gurl fiv yers old and she is going to nit lots more for the dere soljers."

I hope the soldier who got these stockings was one who had a little girl at home himself. Then I am sure he would understand what hours and hours of hard work this baby girl had put into this pair of socks.

Another little girl, Emma Andrews, only ten years old, used to come to the rooms of the Society in her town every Saturday and fill her basket with pieces of linen which had been sent in for bandages for the wounded soldiers. These she would take home, and cut up into nice towels or handkerchiefs, or roll them into neat bandages, and bring them back the next week. Her busy little fingers made over three hundred towels, all neatly hemmed and folded.

It is said that counting up all the money the children saved, together with the value of their work, they as good as sent over a hundred thousand dollars to aid the Union soldiers during this war.

The very old women, too, some of them so old that they could remember the days of the Revolution even, did their part. Thousands of stockings these half blind old grandmammas would knit, while their thoughts, I fancy, ran back over those years so long ago, when they had seen their fathers go away to fight for this same country in 1812, and in 1775.

One old lady, ninety-seven years old, spun a woollen blanket, and carried it a mile and a half to the Society to send to these soldiers. "It is all I could do," said she; "and I had to bring it myself."

Another old lady, Mrs. Bartlett of Medford, Mass., knit over a hundred and ninety pairs of socks for the Union soldiers.

PROCLAMATION OF EMANCIPATION

Well, children, those words look big enough to take away your breath! They are bigger than "religious persecution," of which we had so much in the colonial times; or, "taxation without representation," "declaration of independence," of which we heard in the Revolution; or, "impressment of American seamen," of which we heard in the war of 1812.

I wish I were not obliged to use any large words in these little histories; but once in a while it seems impossible to do without them. These phrases, with their long words, have been handed down through all these years of our country's history until they have come to be as settled as the name of a city or the name of a river; and someway it doesn't seem as if they ought to be changed, not even for little folks, any more than the names of cities or rivers should be changed.

And there are not many of them after all.

See if you can repeat these words all together.

1. The early settlers in this country left England to be free from "religious persecution."

2. The cause of the Revolution was "Taxation without Representation."

3. The people of this country drew up a paper in which they said they would no longer be ruled over by the English. This was called the "Declaration of Independence."

4. The cause of the war of 1812 was the "Impressment of American Seamen."

5. And now one more: Abraham Lincoln believed that the negro slaves had a right to be free; so he drew up a paper telling them they *should* be free. This was called the "Proclamation of Emancipation."

You remember Gen. Butler had settled the question of what was to be done with the slaves by saying that they were to be taken as "contraband goods," just like so many cattle, or so many barrels of sugar, or bales of cotton.

But there came a time when it was necessary for some law to be made by the government itself in regard to this matter. There needed to be a law regarding the treatment of these slaves which *all* the soldiers should obey: for as it stood now, one general who believed in freeing the slaves would take them into their camps when they fled from their masters, and shield them from harm; while another general, who cared nothing about the slavery question, and was fighting only to save the Union, would let the slave-hunter come into the camp and carry off the poor, black runaways.

The slaves themselves were growing to feel unsafe. They did not know when they fled to the Union camps whether they would fall into the hands of friends or foes.

And so, on *New Year's Day*, 1863, Abraham Lincoln sent out his "Proclamation of Emancipation," saying that from this time forth no man should *own* another man and call him his "slave." The negro was now as free as the white man. No one had now any right to take him away from his wife and his children to be sold, or to carry away his wife and children from him.

Of course, the Southerners were more bitter than ever; and you can hardly wonder that they were. There were men whose regular business had been to buy and sell negroes, just as men now buy and sell horses. They had invested their money in this business, and now, of course, it was all lost. There were others who owned great farms, or plantations as they call them in the South; the work of which had been always done by the slaves. Now these slaves were all free; and, on those plantations where the master had been cruel to them, you may be sure these slaves did not work very long after the news of freedom reached their ears.

We can afford to be generous to these slaveowners even; when we think what a blow it was to them to have their habits of life all broken up in this way. Many of them were as honest as honest can be in believing those black men and women belonged to them; and that they had a right to use them to work their farms. Then, too, there were thousands and thousands of slave-owners who were just as kind to these black people as they were to their own families. Their slaves had their own little cabins, snug and warm, where they could sit happy as children through the long summer evenings, playing their banjos and singing their funny old plantation songs.

Did you ever hear any of these plantation songs? I wish there were room to put five or six of them in this book; for someway, it doesn't seem as if we can have much idea of these simple hearted people unless we hear their songs.

They were such strange people! Ignorant, because they were seldom allowed to learn to read; believing in ghosts and goblins, fond of yelling and singing and dancing, full of strange ideas of the Bible and God and heaven, either hating their masters, as they hated work, or else loving them as a dog loves his master, ready to die for them and the "missus," as they used to call their masters' wives.

You must ask your teachers to read parts of Uncle Tom's Cabin to you, children. In that book you will get an honest story of Southern life, you will read of kind slave-owners, and of cruel slave-owners, of good slaves and of bad slaves; for I don't want you to think, as I did when I was a little child, that all the Southerners were wicked, wicked people, and that all the slaves were whipped and lashed every day of the year. You must remember the Southerners were just as honest in their opinions during the war as the Unionist soldiers were. They were just as brave too; they were ready to suffer everything for their dear States, just as our soldiers were ready to suffer every thing for the Union. You must remember, too, that very, very many of them were kind to their slaves; so kind, that if it were not that these slaves had souls which had the right to grow, minds which had the right to study and learn about the beautiful things of this world—if it were not for these, one might almost think these slaves, many of them, were better off before they were made free. But, it cannot be right for one person to have the *right* to say he *owns* another man, can it? And so because the *principle* of slavery was wrong, it was a grand thing for Abraham Lincoln to come out fairly and squarely and say, "No person in the United States shall hereafter own slaves!"

NEGRO SONG

This is a funny old song that the "darkeys" used to delight to sing in the days when they believed "Father Abraham" was coming to free them.

1. Say, darkeys, hab you seen de mas - sa Wid de mustas on his
2. He six foot one way, two foot tudder, An' he weigh tree hundred
3. De ob - er - seer he make us trou-ble, An' he dribe us round a

face, Go long de road some time dis mornin', Like he gwine to leab de
pound, His coat so big he could n't pay de tai-lor, An' it won't go half way
spell; We lock him up in de smoke-house cellar, Wid de key trown in de

place? He seen a smoke, way up de rib-ber, Whar de Limkum gumboats
round. He drill so much dey call him Cap'an, An' he get so dref - ful
pay; He' s ole enough, big enough, ought to known better Dan to went an' run away.

lay; He took his hat, an' lef ber-ry sudden, An' I spec he 's run a - way!
tann'd, I spec he try an' fool dem Yankees For to tink he 's contraband.
pay; He' s ole enough, big enough, ought to known better Dan to went an' run away.

CHORUS.

De mas - sa run, ha! ha! De dar-keys stay, ho! ho! It

mus' be now de king-dom coming, An' de year ob Ju - bi - lo!

127

FIRST NEGRO REGIMENT

You have not forgotten how short a time ago it was that the anti-slavery men in Boston had been mobbed; you have not forgotten how bitter many Northerners felt towards black men and women, and towards anti-slavery men and women; you have not forgotten the Run-away Slave Law, which allowed a slave owner to pursue his slaves into the Northern States and take them wherever they were found.

All these feelings had been changing little by little during these two years of war. Nowhere was there quite such bitter feeling, and in Boston it seemed to have died away entirely.

Early in this year, after the Proclamation had been sent forth, there began to be much talk of raising a negro army. "Why not let these slaves fight for their own freedom?" the people began to say.

"Niggers can't fight! Niggers don't know enough to fight!" cried some, who did not quite believe in them yet.

"Whoever saw a nigger soldier?" cried another.

"Fancy a nigger trying to Forward, march! Right wheel! Left wheel! Right about Face!" laughed some of the soldiers.

But for all this the "nigger" regiments were formed; and they proved as effective and as brave as those who laughed at them, I have no doubt.

The first regiment of colored men was the Fifty-fourth Massachusetts, Robert G. Shaw its colonel.

This regiment was to have been sent to the capital by way of New York; but it was found that the feeling against negroes was still strong in that city, so strong that there began to be signs of mobs ready to attack this regiment if they passed through that city.

These troops, therefore, were sent by way of water from Boston.

To show you how rapidly the feeling against these black people died out, I must tell you that in only a few months from this time, all New York turned out to cheer a colored regiment that marched down Broadway on its way to the war. Yes, indeed, they were cheered as long, and with as much noise and hearty good-will as had Ellsworth's troops been cheered two years before, when they marched down this same street.

> "To every man upon this earth
> Death cometh soon or late;
> And where can man die better
> Than facing fearful odds,
> For the ashes of his fathers,
> And the temples of his Gods!"
> —*Indiana's Roll of Honor.*

SIEGE OF VICKSBURG

Now that the North had come out fairly, and had, by freeing the slaves, declared one grand principle of Right, we might well expect success to be found on their side; for although it doesn't always look so to us, Good *does* govern, and it gains the victory in the end. In any struggle the man or woman, boy or girl, who knows that his side is the right side, will feel more courage to go on, more surety of success.

ADMIRAL FARRAGUT

And now we shall begin to hear more about Gen. Grant.

Grant's soldiers were mostly men from States up and down the Mississippi. Now, this river, they said, belonged to them. To shut it up, to cut off their trade, would ruin their part of the country; their farms would be of no value, their flocks and herds, their manufactories would be of no value, all because there would be no way of sending their produce to other markets.

"We will fight for this river," said they, "till our blood flows with it to the Gulf of Mexico!"

New Orleans you know, had already been taken by Farragut and Butler. Not far from New Orleans, up the river, was the city of Vicksburg. This was held by the Confederates, and was said to be so strongly fortified that no army in the world could take it from them.

"But it *must* be taken," said Grant. "Holding New Orleans is of no use, if the Confederates just above can keep us from going up and down the river."

"But Farragut and Porter tried to take it after New Orleans; didn't they batter away at it with cannon ball and bomb-shell until they were tired out?" said the doubting ones.

"That makes no difference," said Grant and his men; "Vicksburg *must* be taken!" The city was built on high bluffs which rose straight up from the low flat river bed. All around it were swampy lands, with creeks and little bays, and muddy places where a man would sink in mud over his head; more than this, there were dense tangled forests of hanging moss and brush, with every where fallen trees lying across each other in a way to make it seem almost impossible for an army to get across.

But Grant only knew one thing—that the Unionists *needed* to hold that city. He didn't say very much—Grant never did say very much—but he could think, and think, and think; and after Grant had thought, there was pretty sure to be something done.

The year before, when Farragut had tried to take the city, he had begun cutting a canal through towards it. If this canal could now be finished, ships and gunboats could get around behind the city, and so attack it from the rear.

The soldiers began working at this canal. For several days the work went on, the courage of the workmen rising with every spadeful of earth they threw up; but one day, the ungrateful river, which they were working so hard to save from Confederate hands, overflowed, and away went the banks of the canal, the workmen themselves having to run for their lives.

"The good old river will protect us," said the Vicksburg people; but I'm afraid the river neither knew nor cared very much about either Unionists or Confederates; for it seemed always ready to cut its pranks and capers, first on one side, then on the other.

After this, Grant gave up the canal plan. He had another however, and began at once to carry it out. Marching towards the city to attack it from the rear, he learned that a Confederate force was behind him.

"I leave no enemy in the rear," said Grant. "I do not propose to be shut in here like a rat in a trap," said he; so back he marched, to attack the enemy in the rear. The enemy, however, knew too well they could not withstand an attack, so they fled. The Union soldiers ran up the Union flag on the state-house of the city which the Confederates left, sang a good old battle-song, and then marched back again to meet the enemy coming from the opposite direction.

Half-way between Jackson and Vicksburg, the armies met in battle. The Confederates, driven back into the city, shut themselves up, and waited to see what Grant would do.

Grant made one attack on the city, but it was useless. Now if that other army did not come and attack them, Grant was sure that he could in time starve out the city. So he settled his army round about, and the whizzing of bombs and shells into the city was the only sign of war.

Inside the city the people had dug caves, and had taken their food and furniture into them, that they might be safe from the shells.

In time, however, provisions began to grow scarce. The people had already begun to eat horses, and rats even. Their only hope was that some Confederate force would come and attack Grant. Grant's only hope was that some Confederate force would not come to attack him.

No force came; and in July a white flag was seen floating from the walls of the city. This of course meant, "We can hold out no longer."

On the Fourth of July, the Confederate army marched out, each man throwing down his gun and knapsack as he passed. The Union soldiers stood quietly by as the beaten army passed; but when later they marched into the city, and ran up the Union flag, then cheer on cheer rent the air. This was the happiest "Fourth" the country had seen for a long time.

All this time Gen. Banks had been besieging Port Hudson, just below Vicksburg. But as soon as word came that Vicksburg had surrendered, the commander within Port Hudson knew that all was over. He, too, surrendered; and now the Mississippi was free from its source to its mouth. Every point was in the hands of Union soldiers; and from every fort and from every city floated the Union flag.

"STONEWALL JACKSON" IS KILLED

I almost dread to take you back to see what the army of the Potomac has been doing all this time. While this Army of the West had been so full of success, the Eastern army had met only with defeat.

McClellan, you remember, had been taken from the command, and Burnside had been put in his place. Burnside had made that one unfortunate attack upon Lee in Fredericksburg, and had then settled down in huts by the river side for the winter. Burnside had never felt that he was equal to the guiding of such an army, and now at the beginning of this year, 1863, he resigned his position; and Gen. Hooker—called "Fighting Joe"—was given the command.

Gen. Hooker was wide awake. He began at once getting the army in training for a new start.

His first move was to quietly cross the river, and creep up to Lee's army in Fredericksburg. This he did with such success, that Lee knew nothing about it, till he heard the army at Chancellorsville, just outside of Fredericksburg.

Lee did not care to he attacked in the city; so he marched out to meet Hooker. This attack was managed by "Stonewall Jackson," the General whose very name the Union soldiers had learned to fear.

All day long the battle raged; and a sad day it was for the Union soldiers. Just at its close, Jackson, who had been the very life of the battle, was hurrying towards a company of his own men, when they, mistaking him in the smoke and fire of the battle for a Union man, fired upon him. He was terribly wounded; but, lived on for several days, full of hope to the very last that he should yet be able to take his place again in the battle field.

When Lee heard that Jackson had lost his left arm he wrote to him, "You have lost your left arm; but I, in losing you, have lost my right arm."

Indeed, the loss of Stonewall Jackson was a death blow to Lee, and to the Confederate cause. Gaining ten battles could not make up for it. Jackson, sturdy old soldier that he was, believing fully in the Confederate side, loving his State flag with all his heart, was indeed the General of the Confederates. Wherever he was, rallying his men, there was sure to be victory. Powerful, honest, brave soldier that he was, it seems a pity that his life should have been lost in fighting for a wrong cause.

STORY OF STONEWALL JACKSON

Stonewall Jackson's victories in the Valley had won him great renown. Everybody was anxious to see him, but he was so retiring in his habits that he shunned the public gaze. His dress was generally so shabby that many did not know him, even when they saw him on his old sorrel horse. Once, about the time he joined Lee's army, he was riding with some of his officers through a field of oats. The owner ran after them in a rage, demanding Jackson's name, that he might report him at headquarters.

"Jackson is my name, sir," replied the general.

"What Jackson?" inquired the farmer.

"General Jackson."

"What! Stonewall Jackson!" exclaimed the man in astonishment.

"That is what they call me," replied Jackson.

"General," said the man, taking off his hat, "ride over my whole field. Do whatever you like with it, sir."

BATTLE OF GETTYSBURG

We now come to the battle of Gettysburg. It is the battle of which you will hear, I think, more than all the rest put together. There is a writer who has written a book about the fifteen greatest battles in the history of the whole world; and he has called this battle of Gettysburg one of those fifteen.

Now, it is not that this battle was of itself so very different from any other battle; it was not that the armies were so very much larger; not that the soldiers were so very much braver, or the generals so very much wiser. Still it is spoken of as *the* battle of the Civil War.

Let me try to help you to see just why, then, this was such a great battle.

Lee had now defeated the Union soldiers so many times that he began to think his own army was equal to anything. And well he might; for had he not defeated McClellan and Pope and Burnside and Hooker—four of the greatest generals of the Union army.

BATTLE OF GETTYSBURG

"Now," said Lee, "it is time for us to start again up through Pennsylvania, to New York, and on to Boston if we see fit." Again the Southerners began to make their threats of how the New York streets should soon be rivers of blood, and how proud old Boston should bow before the Confederate army.

The people of Pennsylvania were filled with fright. There was the great Potomac army, made up of the bravest of the North; but never yet had a General been found in whom the people trusted. Nothing but defeat after defeat had been their share. Now, indeed, had come a time when if ever a wise leader was needed, it was needed now. Lee was setting out upon his march into the very heart of the North! What if no one could stop him! What if he went on and on, burning the towns as he passed and taking the people prisoners! When would he stop! What would be the result!

Suppose, children, a great fire should start in the fields and forest outside your town, and come leaping on, burning the grass, the bushes, the trees, the fences—everything in its track, until it reached the rows of houses just on the edges of your town. Now suppose the flames were no redder, the fire no hotter, the smoke no blacker than when it all came rolling over the hills and across the fields. Still, can't you see why just here you would be more frightened, why the firemen would work harder than ever, why the peril, the danger, would be greater than at any time before? Not that the fire is any wilder, but because it had reached that point, where, if it isn't conquered at once and there, the whole town will be lost.

This is just the condition the North was in at the time of this battle of Gettysburg. Gettysburg was like the rows of houses along the edges of the town. Lee's fire had come on and on, sweeping everything before it up to just this point. He was now upon the border-land of the North. A battle was at hand! He, *must* not be allowed to come one step farther! "If we only had a leader!" cried the people. "If we only had a leader!" cried the soldiers. And a leader came. Hooker and another General had a quarrel just about this time over some war question; Hooker threw up the command, and Gen. Meade was put in his place. Meade, with new forces from the North, started on in pursuit of Lee.

When Lee found that so large an army was at his heels, he thought the best thing he could do would be to stand still, and let Meade overtake him. A battle was sure to come sooner or later, and Lee was wise enough to know that the sooner it came, the better; for in case of his own defeat, he would not be far from his own part of the country, and therefore not far from help.

GEN. MEADE

So it happened that Meade came upon Lee at Gettysburg. Gettysburg was a pretty little village, nestling down among the hills; its people so quiet and peaceful—its farms so broad and green—doesn't it seem a shame to fill this beautiful valley with the roar of cannon and the fire and smoke of battle?

The battle began on the morning of the 1st of July. For two days it seemed as if again Lee was to win; but on the third day the tide turned. More than forty thousand men lay dead and wounded on the field. At the close of this third day, Lee began to draw away his forces. Lee was at last defeated. And on the Fourth of July, the same day that Grant's men were cheering within the walls of Vicksburg, Lee's army, what there was left of it, was marching away towards the South, broken, discouraged, defeated; and the North once more was saved.

JOHN BURNS: JENNY WADE

Most of the people of Gettysburg left their homes on the approach of the Confederates, but among the citizens was one old man named John Burns, a veteran of the war of 1812, who had no notion of running away. When he heard that the enemy was marching on the town, he took down his old State musket and began running bullets.

"What are going to do with those bullets?" asked his wife, who had anxiously watched his movements.

"Oh," replied he, "I thought some of the boys might want the old gun, and I'm getting it ready for them."

When the Union troops passed through the streets, he seized his gun and started out.

"Where are you going?" called the old lady after him.

"Going to see what's going on," he answered.

Going to a Wisconsin regiment, he asked the men if he might join them. They gave him three rousing cheers and told him to fall in. A rifle was given him in place of his old gun, and the old man fought bravely in the first day's fight, and received three wounds. When the Union troops fell back, he was left with the other wounded on the battle field, where he was found by the Confederates. Being in citizen's dress, he knew they would shoot him if they found out that he had been fighting against them, so when they said to him, "Old man, what are you doing here?" he replied:

"I am lying here wounded, as you see."

"But what business had you here, and who wounded you, our troops or yours?"

"I don't know who wounded me; I only know that I am wounded and in a bad fix."

"Well, what were you doing here? What business had you here on the field in battle time?"

He told them he was going home across the fields, and got caught in the scrape before he knew it. They asked him where he lived, and carried him home and left him there; they suspected him, for they asked him many more questions; but old Burns stuck to his story, and they finally left him.

There was a heroine as well as a hero among the people of Gettysburg. Before the battle, Jenny Wade was baking bread for the Union soldiers. She was in a house within range of the guns. When the Confederates drove the Union troops through the town, and forced them to take refuge on Cemetery Hill, they ordered her to leave.

But she refused and kept at her work even while the battle was going on. While busy with her baking a Minie ball killed her almost instantly. She was laid in a coffin which had been prepared for a Confederate officer, slain about the same time, and now lies on Cemetery Hill, where the battle raged hottest that day.

"DRAFTING"

How many Northern men had already fallen on the battlefield, do you suppose? I am sure I don't know; and you would have no idea of what the number meant, if I could give it to you. More men, than all the people you ever saw in all your lives, children. If you were to count every man and every woman, every boy and every girl in your city, all the people you ever saw on the cars, all the people you ever saw in the stores at Christmas time, or at the beach in the summer time—if you were to count them every one, even then you wouldn't have, I think, more than a handful compared with the thousands and thousands of Northern men who had gone to join the army.

And for two long years they had been fighting, with no success of much importance until the taking of Vicksburg and the driving back of Lee from Gettysburg.

Do you wonder, then, that at the beginning of this third year of the war, there were so few men left in the North and many of those so discouraged that Lincoln could no longer depend upon volunteers. Do not forget, children, that up to this time, all these brave men had joined the army of their own free will. They need not have gone had they not wanted to—nobody had made them go. They had gone bravely, because they thought it was *right*, and because they so loved their country that they were willing to give up friends, home, family—everything, and die, if need be for their Flag.

But now, in this third year of the war, the President was forced to "draft" these northern men—that is, he had to say to each town, you *must* send so many men.

This draft was made as mild as possible. No men over forty-five years of age were drafted, and no boys under eighteen. No son who had a widowed mother depending upon him, nor a father who had motherless children. You see, every attempt was made not to be unjust or cruel in this drafting.

There was in the North, at this time, a party who called themselves the peace party. They were tired of the war, had lost their courage by these two long years of defeat, and said the best thing that could be done was to declare peace, and let the Confederate States do as they pleased. This sounds all very well; but I am sure even you children can see that it was too late to talk that way then, and it was by far too early to say to the South, "You have beaten us; we give up the struggle."

These "peace-party" men managed to stir up a good deal of anger among the low, ignorant classes in the city of New York, and a terrible riot followed. On the day the "drafting" began in that city these low people formed themselves into a mob—as they had done once before perhaps you remember—and, half drunk, armed with clubs and knives, they surged up and down the streets, killing policemen, stabbing and trampling upon black men and women and children, burning their bodies, or dragging them through the streets. Houses were entered, stores were robbed, and buildings burned.

For three whole days, this horrible riot went on—till, at last, a band of soldiers arrived. Then the mob, cowards, as such people are, slunk away to their dens and their grog-shops, and the riot, one of the most terrible and most disgraceful events of the war, was at an end.

ATTACK ON CHARLESTON

From the very beginning everyone knew that if Richmond and Charleston could be taken, and the Mississippi be freed from the control of the Confederates, the war would be at an end. The Mississippi was already free, and it seemed high time that something be done towards taking Richmond and Charleston.

Charleston is a sea-port on the coast of South Carolina. It has a fine harbor, just outside of which are many small islands. The Confederates knew this was one of their strong-holds, and they had taken great pains, therefore, to guard it. On each of these little islands was a fort; and right in the middle of the entrance to the harbor stood old Fort Sumter, its Confederate flag flying, as proud and grand as you please. This fort, you remember, had been taken by the Confederates at the very beginning of the war.

You can see how impossible it would be to enter that harbor, with all its forts ready to aim their guns upon any vessel that should dare attempt it. Indeed, one might as well have tried to enter a hornet's nest as to enter this harbor with any common kind of vessels.

It has always been a wonder to me that after that little Yankee cheese-box did such wonderful work, there weren't twenty more of them built and sent straight down to this harbor. But all this time nothing of very much importance had been done, and Charleston had good reason to suppose that it would not be taken.

Early in this year of 1863, an attempt was made to enter this harbor. Commodore Dupont, with five gun-boats and nine "Monitors," steamed in between two of these islands, and began pouring their fire upon Fort Sumter. But with all these forts filled with soldiers and guns as they were now, it is hardly to be wondered at that the attack was a failure. Even the nine little Monitors steamed back out of the harbor as fast as ever they could, while the Charleston people from the tops of their houses looked on with delight at the whole proceeding. They were sure their harbor could not be taken now!

Later, another attack upon the city was made. This time with double forces. While a fleet was to attack them from the waterside, land forces were to attack them from the rear. On Morris Island was Fort Wagner, one of the strongest of the Charleston forts. Here a force of two thousand landed, and quietly creeping toward the fort, made an attack upon it. They were driven back; and, hiding in the swamps, waited for more troops to come. A few days later, another attack was made. This time, six regiments went against the fort—among them this first colored regiment, with brave Robert Shaw as its leader.

"Now, my good men," said he to his colored soldiers, "now has come a time for you to prove that freedom is worth the price we pay for it."

On the half-run these regiments advanced. Out came a volume of deadly fire upon them from the fort. On they pressed, leaping the ditches, until at last, scaling the walls, the "Stars and Stripes" were placed upon the ramparts. But only for a second did they stand; the storming column of men fell back, dead; and into the ditch below, fell, too, the flag.

Colonel Shaw had fallen close under the walls; and, when the Union soldiers had all been driven back, and the Confederates came out to bury the dead, they found his body covered over by the dead bodies of his brave colored soldiers whom he had loved so well.

The Confederates boasted that they had "buried him in a ditch under his own niggers;" but no ditch was deep enough to bury the memory of this brave young hero.

This unfortunate attack had proved that Fort Wagner was not to be taken in this manner. The only way now was to try to bombard the fort. But where should they set their cannon, you will ask? Surely not in the water, in front of the fort; and it seemed almost impossible to think of setting up cannon in such a swamp as that in the rear. In a swamp, where, before their eyes, many a workman had sunk out of sight in the slimy mud, seemed hardly a place to plant a cannon.

Still, this they tried to do. Night after night they worked, digging here, and piling up there, until at last

151

they had advanced close upon the fort. Here they drove piles one on top of the other, until a place was made so firm and strong, that a cannon could stand with safety. Upon this firm floor, they built ramparts, and set up their cannon.

The soldiers called this their "swamp angel." Bombardment began, and on the 8th of September this plucky little band of workers marched into the fort and set up the Union flag. One fort in Charleston harbor was ours; one step had been taken towards entering the city.

THE GUERILLAS

Out in Kentucky were bands of horsemen called "guerillas." One of their chiefs, John Morgan, had made his name a terror to loyal people.

During this year of the war, he planned a raid into neighboring States, which was worse than any he had ever before attempted. Crossing the Cumberland river with his two thousand men, he marched to a little encampment of two hundred Union soldiers.

"Surrender!" cried Morgan, riding up to the camp.

"If it were not the Fourth of July," said an officer, coolly, "we might think about it; but Union men never surrender on their nation's birthday." And turning to his men, he ordered an attack on Morgan's men. So fierce and quick was the attack that, in spite of their numbers, Morgan thought best to ride away as fast as he could ride.

Morgan then went on to a little fort commanded by Col. Hanson. Here, too, Morgan was met with a volley from the little band within. In this, Morgan's brother was killed. Then Morgan, wild with fury, set fire to the little fort, and Hanson was forced to surrender.

On went Morgan from town to town, and from village to village, stealing, burning, destroying the crops, tearing up railroads and cutting telegraph wires, wherever he went.

But this could not go on forever. When he had gone up in this way to Ohio, the people began to think it was time that something should be done. Troops were raised and sent against him, and when he was all ready to cross over into Virginia to join Lee's army, he found himself hemmed in by Union soldiers. He was made to give up his arms and be led away a prisoner.

He and his men were taken to a prison, and there, as Morgan himself said afterwards, they were shaved and washed and scrubbed, and put into their cells by a "nigger."

There was another guerilla raid after Morgan's capture. This one was led by a ruffian named Quantrell. He went over into Kansas and fell upon the town of Lawrence, the favorite town of "free state" people, since the days of John Brown.

It was a pretty little village, with its churches and school-houses; lying there so peaceful and quiet on this Sabbath morning!

Into this town rode the ruffian band, Quantrell at its head. This was a most brutal and cowardly attack. Worse than Morgan's even; for his had been upon soldiers usually. This was upon a quiet little village of unarmed men and women. The ruffians burned the houses, robbed the stores, killed men, women and children. It was a disgraceful affair, a cowardly, mean attack upon defenceless people. I am glad, however, that this was not done by any order from the Confederate officers or the Confederate government. It is supposed to have been done by this rough band of men, merely for the sake of plunder, and for their own amusement, if doing such things can be amusement.

BATTLE IN THE VALLEY OF CHICKAMAUGA

The only stronghold now left to the Confederates in the West was Chattanooga. They had been driven from place to place by the Union army, from Kentucky, through Tennessee, until they are now on the very border of Georgia.

You remember, in the first stories of this war, you were told that there were many Unionists in Tennessee; and that it is believed that the State would never have seceded had the Unionists been allowed to speak in the convention which was held there.

You can imagine, then, the delight of these Tennessee Unionists, when Gen. Burnside marched into one of their largest cities, and planted there the Union flag.

It had been a long time since they had seen the good old Stars and Stripes, and it is said that many a one cried for joy when once more they saw the "red, white and blue." On every side, the people crowded around Burnside and his men, offering them food and drink—many of them robbing their own poor homes, that they might bring something to the Union soldiers.

Meantime, Rosecrans, our Union general, followed Bragg, the Confederate general, on to Chattanooga, a little town, lying in a sort of gateway between the mountains, and very nearly on the border line between Tennessee and Georgia.

Both Bragg and Rosecrans knew that here would be a final battle, which would decide who should hold Tennessee—the Confederates or the Unionists. Bragg, therefore, had sent for help to all the other generals round about; and now he had an army far outnumbering the Union army.

A terrible battle was fought here in this beautiful valley of Chickamauga, in which our army was sadly defeated. Rosecrans retreated, leaving 16,000 dead and wounded upon the field.

Rosecrans, although he was a brave general, and had been very successful before, was blamed for having lost this battle, and General Thomas was put in command.

Grant, the quiet general who smoked so much and talked so little, was now in command of all the Western forces. He came to Chattanooga now to see for himself how matters stood. Before he could go to Thomas, he telegraphed, "Hold Chattanooga." The reply that Thomas sent will show you somewhat of the firm character of the man. "I will hold it or starve."

JOHNNY CLEM

Johnny Clem was an Ohio boy, twelve years old. At the battle of Chickamauga, Johnny was in the thickest of the fight. Three bullets went through his cap, but Johnny didn't care for that.

After the battle, when every one was hurrying to and fro, Johnny became separated from his comrades, and was running, gun in hand, across an open field.

A Confederate officer, seeing him, sprang upon his horse and rushed after him.

"Stop! you little Yank!" called the Colonel.

Johnny, seeing that the Colonel was sure to overtake him, halted, faced around to meet the Colonel, and set his gun ready to shoot.

"You are my prisoner, young chap," said the Colonel as he rode up.

But instantly Johnny drew up his gun and fired. The colonel fell dead, and Johnny ran on to join his comrades.

Johnny, for this deed, was made a sergeant, and was put on duty at headquarters. He must have been a very odd-looking little sergeant, I think, dressed in a full sized man's uniform. But perhaps he did have a uniform that fitted him after that; and very likely he made a very spruce-looking sergeant.

"BATTLE IN THE CLOUDS"

Thomas's army had now grown quite large. Sherman had joined him, and Hooker had joined him—both able generals, and both in command of brave soldiers.

Bragg's army lay on Missionary Ridge and on Lookout Mountain. They had enjoyed their position up there greatly. Those on Lookout Mountain could look down upon the Union soldiers, and, with their field glasses, tell every move they made.

This was all very well in pleasant weather, under a cloudless sky; but there came a day, so "misty moisty" that the Unionists could not look up the mountain, neither could the Confederates look down.

Did you ever see a mountain with its summit all lost to sight in a big cloud of mist and rain? The little boys and girls who have lived all their lives close to the beautiful hills, have seen this hundreds of times. It is nothing new to them; but I hope they will never grow to be so used to it that they think it not worth noticing. It is, I almost think, the most beautiful sight in nature. I shall never forget the first mountain I ever saw. It

160

was away down in Maine, up close to the New Hampshire line. As our train steamed out of the forests round a curve, we came all at once upon a broad clear place, with the mountains straight ahead. It was a heavy, cloudy "dog-day" in August;—one minute it would be dark and rainy, with big black clouds overhead, and the next minute, perhaps, the sun would be shining out from the rifts in the very blackest of the clouds. It was in one of these sunshiny minutes that I caught this first glimpse of the mountains. On one of them, settled way down half-way to its base, was a black, black cloud. Above this cloud, the mountain peak stood out bright and clear, in the sunshine. On the side of the mountains, in the cloud, was a rift. Slowly this opened, letting in the sunlight, and showing a little white cottage, nestling there among the trees. Then it closed again, and nothing was to be seen but the black circle of cloud. The light from the top slowly died away, the rain fell, and all was dark again. For a few minutes I felt dazed; it seemed as if I had been dreaming; indeed, it seemed almost as if I ought to rub my eyes to see if I really were not half asleep.

Now, it was just such a day as this, I fancy, that the Battle of Lookout Mountain, or, as we call it, the "Battle in the Clouds," took place.

Hooker started up the mountain to attack Bragg's force. It must have been a strange sight from the valley to watch these men go up, up, higher and higher, until they were lost to sight in the mountain mist.

It was a strange sight to Bragg's army, too, I imagine, when, on the other side of the mist, these blue-coats suddenly came into view.

We often hear people say, "Why, where did you come from? Did you drop from the clouds?" I never heard that Bragg said this to his unexpected visitors, but I'm sure he was surprised enough to have said it.

Grant, from a hill near by, watched the troops climbing up the mountain side until they were lost in the mist. After that, now and then, the clouds would break away, as if to give the watcher a peep at the battle going on. But little use was that after all, for no one could tell which side was winning. It was an anxious time indeed. At last, out burst the gray-coats from the cloud; down the mountain, pell-mell over the river they went—the blue-coats close at their heels. "The gray-coats are running! The gray-coats are running! The Union soldiers are driving them down the mountain!"

The gray-coats were indeed running; and they did not stop until they were safely over the river, and had joined their comrades on Missionary Ridge.

Night had now fallen, and Hooker must wait until morning to follow them farther. When morning came, it was found that the enemy had destroyed the bridge, and were now centered on Missionary Ridge.

Sherman advanced first upon them, and had a sharp fight of it for eight or nine hours. Then Sheridan came to his aid. Again they charged up the mountain side, and again the enemy fled into the valley below. Now Lookout Mountain, Missionary Ridge (so called because there had once been an Indian mission school on its brow), and Chattanooga Valley, all were in the hands of the Union soldiers.

On the following morning, again Sherman and Hooker set out in pursuit of the flying enemy. The contest for Tennessee was now over,—the Confederates were indeed driven beyond its limits, and far into Georgia.

Quite a difference, children, between the quick, active following up of battle after battle under these generals, and the slow, crawling movements of the Army of the Potomac under McClellan.

"We don't propose," these generals used to say, "to give the enemy time to get rested and fed—and so ready to fight us again the next day. No! we are upon them *at once*—before they have time to get back their breath from running."

LIBBY PRISON

I wish there were no need of my saying anything to you children about the horrible life of our soldiers in this Southern prison. If not telling it to you would make it any less a part of the history of this war, I would gladly leave it out of our stories; but it *is* a part of it, and one view of the war would be wholly lost to you if I were not to tell you of these "prison pens," as they were called.

When any of the enemy are captured in a battle, they are, as you know, called "prisoners of war." We say, in a certain battle, so many soldiers were killed, so many wounded, and so many taken prisoners.

In the city of Richmond, that capital of the Confederates, which months and months ago some of our Union generals ought to have "taken prisoner,"— in this city of Richmond stood the "Libby Prison."

It was a large brick building, which, before the war, had been used as a storehouse. It was large, to be sure; but no building is very large when you think of packing thousands and thousands of men into it.

I am afraid these men, packed into this prison like cattle into a freight car, suffered more than you or

I can imagine from filth and bad air, and hunger and starvation. When this building was full, prisoners were confined, on a small island in the James River, called Belle Isle, where a kind of camp was made, surrounded by a wall of earth and by ditches. It is said that the prisoners were penned up there like sheep, without any shelter even in winter, and that many were frozen to death. It is also said that all the prisoners were given poor food, and that they were starved by the Confederates so as to make them unfit for further service. Southern writers say, on the contrary, that these stories are untrue; that the prisoners on Belle Isle were furnished with tents like those of the soldiers who guarded them; and that the food furnished to them and to those in Libby Prison was the same as the rations of their soldiers in the field. They also say that the healthfulness of the place and the good care taken of the prisoners is proved by the fact that out of more than twenty thousand prisoners confined on Belle Isle, only one hundred sixty-four died between June, 1862 and February, 1865, or about five each month.

Whether this charge was true or not, we do not know, but it was believed to be true then. In the early part of 1864, there was an attempt made by Gen. Kilpatrick and Col. Dahlgren, to free these prisoners. It was an unfortunate sort of a plan—one that did more harm than good. With a small band of mounted soldiers they started on a raid to Richmond. They tore up railroads, cut telegraph wires, and did all the mischief they could. When Kilpatrick was within three and a half miles of the city, he halted, expecting to hear Dahlgren's signal from the other side. But he waited in vain. Dahlgren had met only with misfortunes on his march, and was at that moment lying dead in the forests not far distant.

There was great excitement over this affair throughout the country. The Confederates declared that papers were found on Dahlgren's body, showing a plot to free the Union soldiers, and then with their aid, to burn the city and to kill President Davis.

The Unionists declared that this was all a lie, made up by the Confederates to excuse them for treating Dahlgren's dead body as brutally as it is said it was treated when found by the Confederates in the forest.

How much or how little was true on either side, we cannot judge from what was said about it at that time. During a war like this, we should hardly expect to find the people very just in their judgments of each other. The "golden rule" cannot live in war time; and when that is trampled under foot, and hate gets the upper hand, the good angels of peace and truth and justice go away in sorrow, I fear, and leave the field to the bad angels alone.

TRAMP! TRAMP! TRAMP!

In the prison-cell I sit, thinking, mother dear, of you,
 And our bright and happy home so far away,
And the tears they fill my eyes, spite of all that I can do,
 Though I try to cheer my comrades and be gay.

  Tramp, tramp, tramp, the boys are marching,
   Cheer up, comrades, they will come;
  And beneath the starry flag we shall breathe the air again
   Of the freeland in our own beloved home.

In the battle-front we stood when their fiercest charge they made,
 And they swept us off, a hundred men or more;
But before we reached their lines they were beaten back dismayed,
 And we heard the cry of vict'ry o'er and o'er.

  Tramp, tramp, tramp, the boys are marching,
   Cheer up, comrades, they will come;
  And beneath the starry flag we shall breathe the air again
   Of the freeland in our own beloved home.

So within the prison-cell we are waiting for the day
 That shall come to open wide the iron door.
And the hollow eye grows bright, and the poor heart almost gay
 As we think of seeing home and friends once more.

  Tramp, tramp, tramp, the boys are marching,
   Cheer up, comrades, they will come;
  And beneath the starry flag we shall breathe the air again
   Of the freeland in our own beloved home.

OLD VIRGINIA

At the beginning of the war, the governor of South Carolina had said to his people, "In this State we may as well go ahead with our cotton and tobacco planting; for if there is a war the battles will be fought, most of them, up there in Old Virginia on the border line."

This speech of Governor Pickens had come true. As we know, the deadliest warfare had been carried on in the "Old Dominion State," as it is called.

ON TO RICHMOND!

This was the war-cry for 1864. On to Richmond! had been the cry of the Army of the Potomac ever since the war began; but, as we know, that army had never succeeded in getting there.

Now the Army of the West, having swept the enemy all out of Kentucky and Tennessee over into Georgia, set up as their cry, "On to Atlanta!"

Grant, during this time had come to be spoken of in the papers as "that General in the West who talks little, but does much."

"I should like to talk with that little Western General," said Lincoln. "He seems to be the sort of a man to DO." And so it came about that in the spring of 1864 Grant was made Lieutenant-general of the United States armies, and called to take command of the Army of the Potomac.

Grant came. He knew that it was no easy task he had before him; but he knew, also, that this wretched war could be brought to an end speedily if only some one was wise enough to know the way.

After looking over the ground, Grant said, "Our armies have been acting like balky horses—never pulling together. Now I propose to keep close at Lee's heels. I'll hammer and hammer at him until he is all worn out."

Having visited all the armies to know just what sort of soldiers, and what sort of officers he had to deal with, on the 3d of May, 1864, Grant started out to "hammer" Lee. At nearly the same, time Lee started out. The armies met at a place called "The Wilderness." A terrible battle followed,—one of the bloodiest of the war. Grant had begun his "hammering." All day long the armies fought, and when darkness came, fell back, tired indeed; still neither side was ready to yield. During the night aid came to Lee; but, at the same time, Burnside came to the aid of Grant. Lee planned to make an attack upon Grant's army at two o'clock in the morning; Grant also had planned to make an attack upon Lee's army at two o'clock in the morning.

Another day of terrible slaughter followed. Again night fell, leaving two bruised and broken armies, neither willing to admit itself defeated.

After such a battle as this had been the Army of the Potomac had been in the habit of falling back; so, when the order came from Grant to break up camp, the army supposed they were to fall back as usual. But that was not Grant's way. Although he had not defeated Lee, Grant knew that he had greatly shattered his forces. He therefore proposed to go on—the quicker the better.

When it was understood that Grant intended to go on, the soldiers, tired as they were from the long battle, sent up such a chorus of shouts, that you would have thought the very skies would have fallen.

I wonder what Lee thought when he heard those cheers. Surely it didn't sound as if the army was preparing to slink away like whipped dogs.

On the army went, with faces toward Richmond. "Richmond, Richmond, Richmond," was all Grant seemed to think of. If an officer asked, "What for tomorrow, general?" he said, "Richmond." If an officer came to him full of hope and eager to go on, Grant gave him a good hearty handshake, and said, "Richmond, my man!" If an officer came discouraged and doubting, Grant still said, "Richmond."

It was at this time that Grant sent the telegram to Lincoln which became so famous: "*I propose to fight it out on this line if it takes all summer.*"

On the 2d of June another terrible battle was fought at Cold Harbor. Lee, who was now no longer strong enough to make an attack, fell back towards Richmond.

After this battle, Grant decided to take his army across the river, and find the weakest point for attack upon the enemy's forces.

He formed a plan of attack on Petersburg, a place only a few miles from Richmond. As soon as Lee knew what his plans were to be, he poured his army into the city to defend it, and made the fortifications doubly strong.

Grant made one attack upon it, but it was a sad failure. He did not, however, retreat, but settled down before the city, determined to wait for another chance.

Meantime Burnside's soldiers set to work digging out an underground tunnel to one of the strongest forts of the city. For a whole month they worked, planning to undermine it and blow it up with gunpowder. On the 30th of July the mine was exploded. A terrible roar was the first warning to the people in the city. Stones, guns, and pieces of cannon were thrown high in the air. The earth shook as from an earthquake.

When it was over, a great hole like the crater of a volcano was seen in the very middle of the defences. Now came the order to "charge!" But so slowly could they advance over the ruins and heaps of rubbish, that before they were upon the defences the Confederates had rallied from the shock, and were ready to fight like madmen. The crater became to the Union soldiers a "pit of death." The great pit was filled with human bodies, black and white; men, trying to climb from the pit, were driven back with muskets and clubs. It was a scene of horror; and, as Grant himself said, "a needlessly miserable affair."

After this, Grant did little more during the fall and early winter than to hold what he had gained. All this time Sherman had been steadily "marching through Georgia," and on towards Richmond from the South. Everywhere the enemy had retreated before his brave army, and Grant was holding Lee firmly in his grasp at Petersburg.

When January of 1865 dawned, the Southern Confederates knew their end was at hand. Grant, with his persistent "hammering," and Sherman, with his brilliant marching, had indeed drawn their snares close around the Confederate Army.

In March, Lee resolved to make one more attack upon Grant's forces. He hoped to get through Grant's lines and join Johnston's forces in North Carolina. Accordingly, a sudden attack was made, and Fort Steadman, the principal point in all Grant's defences fell into Lee's hands.

Grant was indeed surprised. But soon the Union soldiers rallied, and the Confederates were driven back with great loss of men.

Grant, now that the weather was growing warm, and the muddy bogs and roads were becoming firm and dry, sent word to Sheridan that he had now made up his mind to end this matter. Sheridan, always full of hope and bravery, and quick to move, hastened to Grant's quarters with fresh troops from West Virginia.

Lee's forces were stretched in a circle forty miles around Richmond; but the lines were very thin, and Grant made up his mind that it was time to attack them. Sending Sheridan with horsemen to a place called "Five Forks," where Lee's force was especially weak, he himself began his "hammering," as he still called it, on Petersburg.

Lee was in a fix! He needed all his forces at Petersburg. and he needed them all at Five Forks. At four o'clock in the afternoon of April Fool's Day, the charge was made. The Confederates fought bravely enough. Had their cause been a just one, they had certainly deserved to win. But there was no hope! Soon they were in full flight, Sheridan's cavalry at their heels.

Lee was a brave, wise general. He was a hard man to conquer, but he knew when he was conquered. "Leave Richmond at once," he telegraphed to Jefferson Davis, when his soldiers came flying into Petersburg with the news of their defeat.

The telegram reached Davis the following morning, Sunday, and was carried to him at church. Davis rose and quietly left the church. No one knew what the telegram had told him; nor did he intend they should until he had satisfied himself there was no help. Not until afternoon did he allow it to be generally known that the city was lost. The people knew a battle had been going on; but battles as near as Richmond had gone on before when McClellan was in command, and no harm had come to their city from it.

SHERIDAN'S RIDE

Up from the South, at break of day,
Bringing to Winchester, fresh dismay,
The affrighted air with a shudder bore,
Like a herald in haste to the chieftain's door,
The terrible grumble and rumble and roar,
Telling the battle was on once more,
And Sheridan twenty miles away.

And wider still those billows of war
Thundered along the horizon's bar,
And louder yet into Winchester rolled
The roar of that red sea, uncontrolled,
Making the blood of the listener cold
As he thought of the stake in that fiery fray,
And Sheridan twenty miles away.

But there is a road to Winchester town,
A good, broad highway, leading down;
And there, through the flush of the morning light,
A steed, as black as the steeds of night,
Was seen to pass as with eagle flight;
As if he knew the terrible need,
He stretched away with his utmost speed.
Hill rose and fell; but his heart was gay,
With Sheridan fifteen miles away.

Still sprung from those swift hoofs, thundering south.
The dust, like the smoke from the cannon's mouth,
Or the trail of a comet sweeping faster and faster,
Foreboding to traitors the doom of disaster;
The heart of the steed and the heart of the master
Were beating like prisoners assaulting their walls,
Impatient to be where the battle-field calls.
Every nerve of the charger was strained to full play,
With Sheridan only ten miles away.

Under his spurning feet the road
Like an arrowy Alpine river flowed;
And the landscape sped away behind
Like an ocean flying before the wind;
Swept on with his wild eyes full of fire.
And the steed, like a bark fed with furnace fire.
But lo! he is nearing his heart's desire;
He is snuffing the smoke of the roaring fray,
With Sheridan only five miles away.

The first that the General saw were the groups
Of stragglers, and then the retreating troops.
What was done—what to do—a glance told him both;
Then striking his spurs, with a terrible oath,
He dashed down the line, 'mid a storm of huzzas,
And the wave of retreat checked his course there, because
The sight of the master compelled it to pause.
With foam and with dust the black charger was gray.
By the flash of his eye, and his red nostril's play
He seemed to the whole great army to say
"I have brought you Sheridan all the way
From Winchester down to save you the day!"

Hurrah, hurrah, for Sheridan!
Hurrah, hurrah, for horse and man!
And when their statues are placed on high,
Under the dome of the Union sky—
The American soldier's Temple of Fame,—

There, with the glorious General's name,

Be it said in letters, bold and bright:
    "Here is the steed that saved the day
By carrying Sheridan into the fight,
    From Winchester, twenty miles away!"
          —T. BUCHANAN REED.

SHERIDAN TURNING THE TIDE OF BATTLE

EVACUATION OF RICHMOND

A Richmond newspaper at that time, writing of this day, said:

"It was late in the afternoon before the people really began to know that their city was indeed lost to them. Wagons on the streets were being hastily loaded with boxes, trunks, etc., and driven to the Danville depot. . . . Carriages suddenly arose to a value that was astounding; and ten, fifteen, and even a hundred dollars was offered for a carriage. Suddenly, as if by magic, the streets became filled with men, walking as though for a wager, and behind them excited negroes with trunks, bundles and luggage of every description. All over the city it was the same—wagons, trunks, band-boxes, and their owners, filling the streets. The banks were all open, and people were as busy as bees removing their money. Hundreds of thousands of dollars of paper money were destroyed, both State and Confederate. Night came, and with it came only worse confusion. There was no sleep for human eyes in Richmond that night.

"The City Council had met in the evening and resolved to destroy all the liquor in the city, to avoid the temptation to drink at such a time. About the hour of midnight the work commenced, under the direction of citizens in all the wards. Hundreds of barrels of liquor were rolled into the streets and the heads knocked in. The gutters ran with liquor freshet, and the fumes filled the air. Fine cases of bottled liquors were tossed into the street from third-story windows and wrecked into a thousand pieces. As the work progressed some straggling soldiers, retreating through the city, managed to get hold of a quantity of the liquor. From that moment law and order ceased to exist. Many of the stores were robbed, and the sidewalks were covered with broken glass, where the thieves had smashed the windows. The air was filled with wild cries of distress or the yells of the robbers.

An order had been issued from Gen. Ewell's headquarters to fire the four principal tobacco ware-houses in the city. The ware-houses were fired. The rams in the James River were blown up. The Richmond, Virginia, and another one were all blown to the four winds of heaven.

"The bridges leading out of the city were also fired, and were soon wrapped in flames.

"Morning broke upon a scene such as those who witnessed it can never forget. The roar of an immense conflagration sounded in their ears, tongues of flame leaped from street to street."

By seven o'clock, Monday morning, the Confederate troops were out of the city, leaving Richmond in flames. The streets were still filled with crowds of men and women, black and white, loaded down with their plunder from burning houses and stores.

Here was a negro with a bag of coffee or of sugar upon his back; another with a bag crammed with shoes or hats; a third with several pieces of cotton or woollen cloth on his head, or with an armful of ready-made clothing; a woman with a dozen hoop-skirts; and even children with boxes of thread, ribbons, and other small goods. The Babel of their voices was almost drowned in the roar of the flames and the explosion of gunpowder. Capitol Square was crowded with frightened women and children, huddled among piles of furniture and household goods saved from their burning homes. The Confederate rear-guard had scarcely left when a cry of "The Yankees! the Yankees!" arose in Main Street.

In marched the Union troops. As they entered the city, bursts of cheers went up from each regiment. "Richmond was taken!" and the war was really over.

Lee at once left Petersburg, hastening with his forces towards the West. Grant followed close upon him. There was little need to pursue them; for so broken and exhausted were they, that thousands threw down their arms, too weak and ill to carry them. On the 9th of April, Grant and Lee met, and agreed upon the terms of surrender. It did not take them very long. The "Army of Virginia" was to disband and go home, each man promising to fight no more against the Union.

Lee rode back to his camp, sad and silent. His men received him with a cheer. He looked at them sorrowfully and said, "Men, we have fought the war together; and I have done the best I could for you."

On the 12th of April, the Confederate army came out for its last parade. Grant generously kept his troops out of sight, while Lee's men stacked their guns, and covered them over with the Confederate flags, in sign of surrender.

GUN PRACTICE

FROM ATLANTA TO THE SEA

1. Bring the good old bu - gle, boys! we 'll sing an-oth - er song—
2. How the dark - ies shout - ed when they heard the joy-ful sound!

Sing it with a spir - it that will start the world a - long—
How the tur - keys gob - bled which our com-mis - sa - ry found!

Sing it as we used to sing it, fif - ty thous-and strong,
How the sweet po - ta - toes e - ven start-ed from the round,

CHORUS.

While we were marching thro' Georgia. Hur-rah! hur-rah! We

bring the ju - bi - lee! Hur - rah! hur - rah! the

flag that makes you free! So we sang the cho-rus from At -

lan - ta to the sea, While we were marching thro' Georgia.

ON TO ATLANTA

When Grant took command of the United States' armies, he put William T. Sherman in full control of the "Army of the West."

On the day following the one in which Grant started out for Richmond, Sherman began his march toward Atlanta.

GEN. WILLIAM T. SHERMAN

"On to Atlanta!" was their watch-word, just as in Grant's army, "On to Richmond!" was the watch-word.

I shall not try to tell you of the battle after battle in Sherman's Great March. At Atlanta the enemy drew up all their forces, determined that this place should be fought for inch by inch. It was a hard, close fight, both generals equally wise and brave; but after several days, the Confederate general gave way, and Sherman telegraphed to Grant, "Atlanta is ours, and fairly won."

Hood, the Confederate general wild over the loss of Atlanta, made a desperate dash back towards Nashville, hoping to cut off Sherman's supplies.

Sherman was brave as a lion, but he was also wise as a serpent. He saw at once what Hood was hoping to do. Gen. Thomas, called by his men, "Old Reliable," saved the city. For two days the battle raged: but twilight of the second day saw the Confederates in full retreat. On they went throwing away as they ran, their guns, knapsacks, all that would hinder their flight. Our troops pursued till darkness stopped the race. Next day the pursuit was continued. Thomas strongly hoped to capture all Hood's army. On this point Hood disappointed him. Gathering his troops together, he formed now an orderly retreat, and crossed the Tennessee with what was left of his army. The flight had been indeed Bull Run over again; only this time the Confederates were flying and the Unionists were pursuing.

Sherman feeling sure that Thomas would be equal to any battle with Hood's army, had kept straight on with his plan of marching now "from Atlanta to the sea."

His object was to destroy the railroads, and cut off the supplies of food, clothing, powder and cannon of the Confederate army. This seems almost cruel; but it wasn't half so cruel, in reality, as it would have been to let the war drag on for many months more.

Taking only twenty days' provisions, Sherman told his men they must find their living in the country over which they marched. The men understood what their General meant, and about the middle of November, while Grant was holding Lee's army in Petersburg, Sherman started across "from Atlanta to the Sea."

Just before Christmas, Sherman's army marched into Savannah, and hoisted "Old Glory," as they called their flag. At once he telegraphed to Lincoln, "I beg to present to you as a Christmas present, the city of Savannah, with one hundred and fifty guns, plenty of powder, and twenty-five thousand bales of cotton."

After a long rest, which Sherman's army so greatly needed, and which they so richly deserved, they next moved towards Charleston. The North stood breathless when word came that Sherman was marching towards Charleston. Charleston! the centre of the whole secession country! Charleston! the city that was said to be unconquerable!

But Sherman conquered it, and once more the Union flag waved over old Fort Sumter.

And now the Union Army felt their journey was nearly over. In a few days they would join forces with Grant's own.

Goldsboro' was the next place to fall upon.

Here Gen. Joseph Johnston was straining every nerve for a final battle. It was like a drowning man catching at a straw. He had with him, Bragg from Wilmington, Hardee from Savannah, Beauregard from Charleston, and Wade Hampton, with his cavalry. The shattered remnant of Hood's army from Nashville had joined him.

But affairs looked dark for the Southerners. Their army in Tennessee had been broken up, Lee was held by Grant in Virginia; Sherman had conquered Georgia and South Carolina; if he now joined Grant, Lee's army would be captured. The only hope was that Johnston might defeat one or all of the armies marching on Goldsboro', and prevent their junction with the Army of the Potomac; then go north and help Lee drive Grant from his post near Richmond. It was a desperate last chance, and might be successful.

A bloody battle followed, but when night fell, Sherman's soldiers had not fallen back one inch. During the night several fresh divisions had come and joined the Union soldiers, making our lines now too strong to be broken. Johnston retreated during the night and Goldsboro' was won.

It was not long after this that Johnston surrendered to Sherman, knowing that since Lee had surrendered to Grant, the war was indeed at an end. Johnston accordingly wrote to Sherman asking that there be no further bloodshed between their soldiers, and offering to surrender his whole army.

TORPEDOES

Some very cruel work was done during the war with torpedoes. When Richmond was evacuated, the troops were sent into the city with orders to move very carefully for it was reported that the streets had been filled with torpedoes. You can easily imagine what the explosion of one of these under foot would do. Fortunately, however, when the Confederates had put these torpedoes into the ground, they had marked the location of them all with little red flags, that they themselves might know where *not* to step. In the rush and hurry of leaving the city, these flags had been entirely forgotten. It was very fortunate for the Union soldiers that they had been left standing there, warning them as well as the Confederates where not to step.

Torpedoes were put in the harbors, too. Did you ever see a three-tined prong attached to a torpedo in the water? The prong is fastened to the torpedo in such a way that when a vessel comes sailing along, it would strike against those little hooks. That would move the lever connected with the trigger of the pistol within, and a fearful explosion would be the result. Thousands of brave men's lives have been lost in this cruel way; and if it is a good thing to kill off thousands of men and blow them in pieces, then torpedoes are, I suppose, a very good thing. They are spoken of as one of the improvements of modern warfare. What do you think, boys?

SIGNALS

During the war it was often necessary to signal from place to place.

During the night, signalling was done by torches, during the day, by flags.

Suppose there were two signal parties, on two different mountains, five or ten miles apart. Suppose there is a battle going on near one signal party, or a bridge has been burned, or the enemy are coming near. The other signal party will need to know of all this. So first of all the flag-man sets up his flag. The officer gets his field glass in position, and watches until he finds that the signal party on the other mountain has seen the signal, and is waiting to receive the message.

Now the flag-man begins to signal. He waves his flag to the right, or the left, or the front.

Suppose to the right means 1, to the left 2, in front 3. Now, if the flagman should dip twice to the right, once to the left and once in front, that would make the number 1,123.

When the officer on the other mountain had got the whole signal, he would look in a book he carries, called a "signal code." and learn what 1,123 means.

Perhaps he would find that it meant "railroad bridge burned," or "send us troops at once," or "we have defeated the Confederates," or "Grant is only five miles away."

Of course these books have to be kept very secret; and if in any way one of them should fall into the hands of the enemy, a new set of numbers would have to be made out for it wouldn't be a very nice thing to have the enemy know what the signals meant.

THE WAR IS OVER

Picture to yourself if you can, the joy of the people in the North when the news of these surrenders spread over the land! The telegraphs flashed it over the wires from city to city and from town to town, until the news reached the lonely homes away out on the prairies and away up on the mountains.

Our "Union boys," the "boys in blue" tossed up their hats for joy. Faces in the homes—even in those whose soldier boys would never come back to them—shone with thankfulness that this cruel war was over.

But nobody was happier than Lincoln himself. Washington was all one blaze of light; fireworks were shooting, bonfires were blazing, and bands were playing.

President Lincoln came out upon the balcony of the White House, and asked one of the bands to play the tune of "Dixie." This had been the favorite tune of the Confederates all through the war, just as "John Brown's Body" had been the favorite with our soldiers.

"I have always thought Dixie one of the best songs I ever knew. Our enemies over the way tried to make it their own; but I think we captured it with the rest; and I now ask the band to give us a good turn on it."

This was Abraham Lincoln's last public speech.

Next evening, the 14th of April, the president went to the theatre to see an English play, called "Our American Cousin." For four years the heavy duties of his great office, the sorrow which he had felt at the horrors of the war, had made an evening of amusement almost impossible for him.

But the war was over; he could lay off some of his cares. There was now to be a little time for laughter and enjoyment; a holiday for the nation and its president. So Mr. Lincoln went to the theatre, sitting in a box just above the stage. About half-past ten o'clock in the evening, as the play drew near its close, a man named John Wilkes Booth, wrapped closely in a cloak, entered the box. He came up behind the president and shot him in the back of the head. The ball entered the brain, Lincoln's head drooped forward, his eyes closed, and he never spoke afterwards. It is hoped that he felt no more pain, though he lingered until next morning, and then quietly passed away.

After the shot the murderer with the cry, "Thus may it be always with tyrants," leaped over the box railing down upon the stage. Rushing hastily through the frightened actors, hardly conscious of what had been done, he escaped through a back entrance, mounted a horse made ready for him at the theatre door, and rode rapidly away.

This news of horror so quickly following that of joy, spread over the country, filling it with gloom. This good, simple man, Abraham Lincoln,—this gentleman of the people,—had won to himself all loyal hearts. His face, so full of pathos, winning in spite of its rugged plainness, his manly, truthful nature; his noble humanity; had gained him the regard even of those who at first sneered at the "vulgar rail-splitter." Across the ocean in England where he had been held up to ridicule, his name was now mentioned with reverence.

The assassin, as he leaped from the box upon the stage, had caught his foot in the American flag, which draped the front of the President's box. He fell forward and broke his leg in the fall. A party was at once sent in pursuit of him. On the 21st of April he was found in a barn near Fredericksburg. Defiant to the last, he stood at bay, like a hunted wild animal, with loaded weapon, prepared to take the life of any one who attempted to take him alive.

The barn was set on fire, and, as he attempted to escape, he was shot at by one of those in pursuit, and so captured. He died soon after from the effects of the wound, and his body was buried secretly.

Andrew Johnson, the vice-president now became president, and the people set to work to bring the country back into its old condition of peace and prosperity. Since then the country has grown very rapidly, and we are to-day the freest, the happiest, the richest, the best nation, I hope you all think, on the face of the earth.

Peace shall unite us again and forever,
    Though thousands lie cold in the graves of these wars;
Those who survive them shall never prove, never,
    False to the flag of the Stripes and the Stars!

WHEN JOHNNY COMES MARCHING HOME

1. When John - ny comes marching home a - gain, Hur - rah, hur-
2. The old church bell will peal with joy, Hur - rah, hur-

SOLO.   CHORUS.

rah! We'll give him a heart - y welcome then, Hur - rah, hur-
rah! To wel - come home our dar - ling boy, Hur - rah, hur-

SOLO.

rah! The men will cheer, the boys will shout, The
rah! The vil - lage lads and las - sies say, With

CHORUS.

la - dies, they will all turn out, And we'll all feel
ro - ses they will strew the way,

gay when John - ny comes march - ing home.

195

BATTLE HYMN OF THE REPUBLIC

1. Mine eyes have seen the glory of the com-ing of the Lord: He is trampling out the vintage where the grapes of wrath are stored; He hath loosed the fateful lightning of His ter-ri-ble swift sword: His truth is march-ing on.

2. I have seen Him In the watch-fires of a hun-dred circling camps; They have builded Him an al-tar in the even-ing dews and damps; I can read His righteous sentence by the dim and flar-ing lamps: His day is march-ing on.

Glo - ry, Glo - ry, Hal - le - lu - jah,

Glo - ry, Glo - ry, Glo - ry, Hal - le - lu - jah, Glo - ry

Glo - ry, Hal - le - lu - jah! And we are marching on.

3 He has sounded forth the trumpet that shall never call retreat;
He is sifting out the hearts of men before His judgment-seat;
Oh, be swift, my soul, to answer Him! be jubilant, my feet!
   Our God is marching on. — Chorus — Glory, etc.

4 In the beauty of the lilies Christ was borne across the sea,
With a glory in His bosom that transfigures you and me;
As He died to make men holy, let us die to make men free,
   While God is marching on.— Chorus — Glory, etc.
      Humming Bird.

197